COMPASS

A Handbook on Parent Leadership

COMPASS

A Handbook on Parent Leadership

James B. Stenson

 Scepter

Other books by James B. Stenson, published by Scepter Publishers

Lifeline: The Religious Upbringing of Your Children

Preparing for Adolescence: A Planning Guide for Parents

Preparing for Peer Pressure: A Guide for Parents of Young Children

Successful Fathers: The Subtle but Powerful Ways Fathers Mold Their Children's Characters

Upbringing: A Discussion Handbook for Parents of Young Children

Anchor: God's Promises of Hope to Parents

Compass: A Handbook on Parent Leadership
Copyright © 2003 James B. Stenson.
All rights reserved

Published by Scepter Publishers, Inc., New York
(800) 322–8773 / www.scepterpublishers.org

ISBN 1–59417–000–2

Text composition in Monotype Baskerville fonts
Printed in the United States of America

Contents

Acknowledgments

More than most other books, *Compass* is the work of many people. It's a composite of many parents' generous contributions. I wish to thank, therefore, the many great men and women whom I've been honored to befriend in my years of teaching and lecturing, people who shared their family-life experiences with me and whose experienced insights form the substance of this work. Much as I would like to honor each of them personally, they are far too many to list here.

I do need to thank some parents for the special help they've given me in assembling material for *Compass*, especially their experiences in running various parent-discussion initiatives. Busy as they are with their growing families, they were generous enough to give time and thoughtful suggestions in response to my many queries. They are John and Ana Marie Abbracciamento, Pat and Theresa Fagan, Maurice and Dianna Gordon, Joe and Lorelei Itchon, Joe and Diane Lechner, Steve and Nancy Markel, Tom and Amy Spence, Jim and Patty Sutterer, and Chris and Anne Wolfe.

I owe special thanks, too, to Kenneth G. Forstmeier of Bellefonte, Pennsylvania, for his extremely helpful insights and constructive suggestions for the text of *Compass*.

Finally, I extend my heartfelt gratitude to the directors of the R. Templeton Smith Foundation of Cleveland Heights, Ohio, whose generous support over several years made this work possible. Without their encouragement and assistance, I could not have undertaken this project nor brought it to completion.

Introduction

What This Handbook Is All About

"I sure wish I had known all this twenty-five years ago!" That's what I've sometimes been told after my conferences on successful parent-leadership, lectures I have given over the past several years to groups of parents throughout the English-speaking world. The words, often said in humor but sometimes with wistful regret, came from older parents, mothers and fathers whose children had already grown and left home.

To come right to the point here: I have written this handbook, the fruit of my thirty years' experience with families, so that you, a young parent, won't have to express this regret in the future. I've written it so that you will form a much clearer idea of how other parents, ordinary men and women just like you, have lived as great leaders in family life and have succeeded with their sacred mission: to raise their children right. I want to give you a "job description," so to speak, on how to succeed as a leader to your children.

Let me be clear here. When I say "succeed," I don't just mean parents' methods of discipline, or how they keep kids under control, or how they handle hassles in family life. These are short-term achievements but only part of real parental leadership.

Parents really win success with their children only in the long term. *Parents succeed with their children when the kids grow up to become competent, responsible, considerate, and generous men and women who are committed to live by principles of integrity—adults who bring honor to their parents all their lives through their conduct, conscience, and character.* Raising children to become adults like this is what parenthood is all about.

Raising children right is difficult these days. It is a real challenge to know what you're doing and where you're going. And as the great Yogi Berra reportedly once said, "If you don't know where you're going, you'll wind up someplace else."

As I hope you'll better appreciate from this book, raising a healthy family is a great sporting adventure. When parents bring children into the world, they set out on the greatest, most satisfying adventure of all—the challenge of leading their children, little by little, day by day, to become great men and women.

To do this right, parents need a compass, some fixed frame of reference to help them cope with uncertainty, set their bearings from time to time, and lead their family confidently. Without this compass to fall back on, parents can easily lose their way in the hectic tangles of normal family life.

So, what is this compass, this set of reference points, that I've seen great parents rely on—and that forms the lessons of this handbook? The compass of great parents is several things:

• Their sense of sacred mission: the certainty that God has called them to lead their children to responsible adulthood, to lead them to have a great life, and to lead them home to Him.

• The compelling and hopeful vision they have of their children's lives twenty years from now, what kind of responsible, competent, upright men and women they should grow to be.

• Their commitment to build character and conscience in their children that will last them all their lives.

• Their reliance on three sources of strength: God's help, their own never-failing love for their children, and the experienced wisdom of other parents who've succeeded.

• Their steely determination, bolstered each day by their

ideals and prayers, never to give up until their children have grown to become excellent men and women.

This book explains details of this compass that great parents live by and succeed with. But that's not all. It sketches out a kind of map for you, too. It shows you the terrain where others have ventured, the day-to-day experiences of other parents who've succeeded with the challenges of family life. Almost everything in these pages comes from parents' experience, much of it hard won.

Let me back up a bit and explain how I came to write this book.

For twenty-one years, I worked to help establish two independent secondary schools, one in Washington, D.C., and the other in Chicago—The Heights School and Northridge Preparatory School, respectively. I was director of Northridge for twelve years. By any measure, I'm pleased and proud to say, both of these schools have been hugely successful. That is, they've turned out excellent young adults who bring honor to their families.

During that time, I made it my business to know hundreds of families intimately. I studied their family lives up close. I watched children grow into maturity, very often successfully but sometimes not. Over many years I talked with hundreds of fathers and mothers, visited their homes, asked questions, learned a lot.

All this I did for one reason: I wanted to learn how parents succeed or fail with their children.

I watched many parents succeed as leaders, while others failed, and their children eventually left our schools. Some parents saw their children mature into excellent men and women, often before they left high school. Others, though, especially as their kids struggled through adolescence and young adulthood, met with disappointment, regret, and even tragedy. Their children suffered from lack of self-confidence and self-control, substance abuse, protracted immaturity, irresponsible and self-destructive behavior, aimlessness in life, troubles with careers or marriages or the law.

Through my countless conversations with fathers and mothers, I tried to account for the differences. I searched for patterns of family life among those people who eventually triumphed with their children. What did these successful fathers and mothers have in common? What was their compass, that set of guiding principles to which they kept referring? What did they manage to do right? Most importantly, what could other parents learn from their experience?

Over the years I learned a lot. As headmaster I worked to pass on this experience to other parents, and many of them were grateful for this help and encouragement. They formed a clearer picture of their job, put the practical lessons to work in family life, and thus found greater confidence in leading their children to form strong conscience and character.

And that's the reason for this book. Its purpose is to help you learn from the successful experience of other conscientious parents, men and women who have succeeded with their children.

It's important for you to understand something at the outset: What I lay out for you in these chapters is *de*scriptive, not *pre*scriptive. That is, I don't claim to have all the answers about family life, and I don't know anyone who does. What I'm doing here is describing the kind of thinking and action— the compass of parenthood—that successful parents have lived by and taught me.

Since you are busy (to say the least), I have made this book short and to the point. As much as possible, I've tried to make it thought-provoking. Clear thought is necessary for any leadership, and especially in family life. Foresight, planning, fixing priorities, clarifying your principles: all these actions are crucial for your confident parental leadership. In other words, knowing where you're going helps you know what you are doing, and this builds the courage you need to stick with your mission, no matter what. A compass like this gives you greater confidence, and confidence is one of the secrets of successful parenthood.

I would urge you—husband and wife—to read this book together slowly and thoughtfully. After each chapter, you will find questions and issues to stimulate your thought. Pick and choose among them; make up questions of your own. Whatever you do, invest the time (and it is an investment, with a big payback) to reflect, talk things over, prod yourselves steadily toward the ideal of parental partners: *unified dual leadership*. Remember that each of your children has only one mind and one conscience, and therefore needs one clear set of directions, and only one, coming from both of you together.

A couple of final points.

As you read this book, you'll notice that some key ideas are repeated. This is unavoidable. Why? Because assessing a complex issue such as family life is like studying a diamond: you turn the jewel around and see the whole through its different facets. Similarly, a family life's dimensions can be scrutinized from different points of view. So please be patient. When you've read *Compass* all the way through, you should see everything fall into place.

Also, a caveat: Please be aware that human nature, endowed as it is with God-given free will, is mysterious and often surprising. We see this in history and in many families today. For instance, Beethoven and Isaac Newton came from dysfunctional families; George Washington and Thomas Jefferson and Alexander Hamilton grew up in single-parent homes. Today, most children from consumerist homes are spoiled, but some are not. Some parents were brought up badly and then spoil their own children in turn; others, though, manage to turn their lives around and then raise their children right.

The upshot is this: for nearly any generalization we make about people, we can cite exceptions. So when this book generalizes about people or family dynamics, please realize that we're dealing here with trends and probabilities, not certainties, and certainly not dogmas or infallible recipes. There are no such formulas or recipes. Human life is ultimately mysterious.

Finally, though this book was written mostly for a husband and wife to read and discuss together, I've also designed it to be used by parent discussion groups. If you're interested in forming such a Compass Group to share experiences and insights with friends—and I urge you to do so—please read the Appendix. It explains people's experiences with running groups of this sort and why many parents today have found this so hugely helpful and encouraging. Getting together to learn with friends—for the long-term welfare of all your children—may be one of the smartest things you've ever done. This is what many parents have told me.

If you wish to receive supplementary information and updated advice on what appears in *Compass*, especially in organizing a Compass Group among your friends, please consult my Website: www.parentleadership.com.

I earnestly wish you every success with your children. I share your hope that they will grow up to be great men and women, adults who will bring you joy and pride in the years to come, your life's reward for all your loving efforts. With the help of the compass described here, may your life together as a loving family be a grand, beautiful adventure.

CHAPTER ONE

The Big Picture: Forming Character

Let's get right to the point here and look at questions that set the points of our compass: What constitutes the vocation of parenthood? What is the mission parents have to carry out with their children? What is a parent for? What is family life really all about?

We should clear up some misunderstandings: The job of parents is not merely to feed, clothe, and shelter their children and provide for their technical education. Nor is it just to keep the kids busily amused and therefore (we hope) out of trouble. Nor is it even to prepare children for later success in highly paid careers. Certainly these tasks need to be done, but they're not enough. Not nearly enough.

Why do we say this? Because, as we see all around us today, plenty of children are supported in these basic ways. They are nourished, clothed, sheltered, amused, and technically well educated. Yet later, in adolescence and in young adult life, they crash headlong into serious personal problems and meet with devastating disasters, even tragedies such as addiction and moral collapse and suicide, which break their parents' hearts.

When all is said and done, the real job of parents is to protect their children from harm, not just now but in the years ahead—in their personal lives, their marriages, their careers, their souls. The big job is to strengthen the children while they're small so they can later protect themselves and their loved ones.

To look at it another way, parents must teach their children to *see the invisible*. Conscientious and savvy parents lead their children to know, and live by, those internal, invisible realities that form a great life: *honor, integrity, self-mastery, courage, courtesy, dedicated service, sacrificial love, conscience, God, grace, the soul.* Great men and women, it seems, are moved mostly by what's invisible.

In short, the real job of parents is to form in their children, for a lifetime, those invisible strengths of mind, will, and heart that collectively we call *character.*

Some parents succeed at forming their children's character. Some do not. This book is all about how smart, savvy parents succeed at their job: how they raise their children to become great men and women, people of character.

But before we delve into details of *how* this is done, we must first stand back and look at the big picture, the *why.* So, we begin by looking at character.

Character: a working description

This invisible thing we call character resides in the mind and will and heart. Like other spiritual qualities we esteem in people—healthy self-confidence, charisma, kindness, honesty, courage, will power, "class"—character is difficult to define but easy to detect. We recognize character when we see it in people, and we grow distressed, or at least uneasy, when we find it missing, especially among those on whom we must depend.

Let's look at some common-sense descriptions; then we can target in with a precise definition.

• Character is what we have left over if we ever go broke. Character is what each of us is, minus our money and possessions.

• Character is the aggregate of qualities that people esteem in us despite our personal shortcomings. Indeed, it's what they admire about us in how we cope with those shortcomings. (For instance, we respect someone who admits he's a "recovering alcoholic" and struggles to overcome his affliction.)

• Character is what people admire in us besides our talents and acquired skills. It's an observable fact that people may display dazzling talents and skills but still lack character. (For example, just read the sports page and look at the glaring personal flaws of gifted athletes. Or just glance around your workplace; the business world suffers no shortage of technically skilled barbarians.)

• Character is what parents seek most in their grown children's prospective spouses. It's what parents want above all among their sons-in-law and daughters-in-law. The prospect of having a son or daughter marry someone without character is every conscientious parent's nightmare.

• Character is what employers hunt for when they read between the lines of job-applicants' résumés and references.

• Character is what makes people proud and delighted to count us as friends, not just acquaintances. It is what makes friendships last a lifetime.

• Character is what children unconsciously imitate in their parents' lives. It is the compass by which they judge their own peers, including prospective spouses.

Because character is so elusive an idea, we need some sort of framework to think about it, a sensible breakdown into constituent parts. Here's one framework that parents have found helpful. It comes with a pedigree more than two thousand years old, for it was originally devised by the Greeks.

The ancient Greeks had a lot to say about character. Removed as they were from our complex world of computers, mass media, and technological gadgets, they formed a clear, unsurpassed vision of human nature. Though the Greeks lived imperfect lives themselves, the best of them thought deeply about ethics, goodness, beauty, and truth. We still turn to them for wisdom because they were so often insightful about human life.

To the greatest minds of antiquity, especially Aristotle, character is an integration of what they termed the "virtues," those powers of mind and will and heart built up through repeated practice: *prudence, justice, fortitude,* and *temperance.* Character, to them, is the sum total of these habitual powers joined together in one's personality. It determines what we are at the center of our very self, our soul. And it directly affects how we go about living with others.

For the sake of clarity, and your confident parental action, we consider the great virtues—that is, character strengths—in more modern-day, commonsensical terms:

- Prudence is *sound judgment and conscience.*
- Justice is *a sense of responsibility and fair play*
- Fortitude is *courage, persistence, "guts."*
- Temperance is *self-mastery, self-discipline, self-control.*

To these four classical concepts of virtue, we add the other, immensely important inner strength drawn from our Judeo-Christian ethic, that of *heart.* (The ancient Greeks were, in many ways, a heartless people.) This is *generosity, magnanimity, charity, a capacity for compassionate understanding and forgiveness.* In religious terms, it is the virtues of faith, hope, and charity—to love and serve God by loving and serving others, starting with family and friends and radiating out to others, all brothers and sisters under our heavenly Father.

At this point, we must lay out a couple of ideas you should grasp at the outset, for they're crucial to your job as a parent.

First, children do not come into the world imbued with these virtues. Surely, small children shine with many beautiful qualities that charm us and move us to cherish them. Most of the time, they desire to please those who love them. They do not bear grudges. They are resilient in bouncing back from adversity, and they are open to wonder and beauty. But let's face it frankly, they do not start out in life with sound judgment, responsibility, courageous perseverance, or self-mastery. These powers must be built from scratch as children grow up—formed, as it were, from the outside in—or else the children will grow up without them.

To look at your challenge another way, children come into the world with the exact opposite of these virtues. Despite their lovable charms and winsome ways and desires to please, children are also driven by fuzzy and emotional thinking, irresponsible self-centeredness, escapism, and a constant drive to self-indulgence. They often live as *me*-centered hedonists, given over to gratifying their passions and appetites at once, and impelled to impose their wills on others around them, sometimes by coy manipulation and occasionally by force.

Anyone who doubts this should talk with any experienced teacher or savvy veteran parent. Or just spend a couple of days monitoring a school playground. Or watch and listen as spoiled youngsters wildly misbehave in stores and restaurants. (Why is it we notice glaring flaws more readily in other people's children?)

The second key point, related to the above, is this: Your job as a parent is to make sure your children do not grow up this way: as thoughtless, self-centered, impulsive, irresponsible hedonists and manipulators. *Your job is to teach your children habitual lifelong powers of sound judgment, responsibility, courageous perseverance, self-control, and heart. This is the core responsibility of parenthood.*

And the universal experience of the human race is this: to fail at this job, to see your sons and daughters grow up with their childhood flaws still intact, all you have to do is . . . nothing.

If you neglect your responsibility as parent, you may find one day (as, tragically, so many parents do) that your children have grown into teens and young adults with their childish faults still firmly in place. Your physically grown-up children could be, at age fifteen or twenty or twenty-eight, just six-foot-high versions of what they were at age two. As teens and young adults, they could still live as self-centered pleasure seekers, dominated by out-of-control appetites (including for drugs), irresolute and irresponsible, and practically incapable of serving other people—even if they wanted to.

Please understand this, for it is vitally important: *Your children will not grow up when they can take care of themselves. They will really and truly grow up only when they can take care of* others—*and want to.*

So, to work change in your children, to lead them to become men and women of strong character, is your great challenge as a parent. It is the greatest responsibility of your life. And, no matter what else you accomplish, to succeed at this, to see your children grow up this way, will be your life's greatest, most satisfying, achievement.

How character is formed

We've sketched the great character strengths in abstract outline here, but they are real. To flesh out your understanding, pause here to reflect about those people you've most esteemed in life: parents, relatives, neighbors, bosses and co-workers, people in public life. List them by name and think about their outstanding qualities.

Didn't you admire them for their character? Didn't they show excellent judgment, wisdom, a refined sense of right and wrong? How did they show their ethical uprightness? Didn't many take their religion seriously, drawing strength from a personal relationship with God? What kind of courage did they bring either to solving problems or living with them patiently? Didn't they show thoughtful concern for others' needs and feelings? Weren't they on top of life, enjoying life to the fullest but without going overboard? Didn't they always seem to put people ahead of things? Weren't they delightful to be with, enjoyable to work with?

Your children can grow up to become like these admirable people. In fact, they must.

How do parents do this? How do young people grow in character at home? The collective experience of family life everywhere shows that children seem to acquire character in three ways, and in this order:

• First, *example*: what children witness, and then imitate, in the lives of their parents and other adults whom they respect (such as excellent teachers and coaches).

• Second, *directed practice*: what children are led to do, or are made to do repeatedly (despite their resistance), by parents and other respected adults.

• Third, *word*: what children hear from parents and others as *explanation* of what they witness and are led to do.

Let's focus on these three ways of acquiring character. They are an outline of your role as an effective parent leader.

Example

You teach character to your children mostly through your own example and, in fact, when you're least aware of it.

You've probably noticed already that children have selective hearing, a kind of filter that screens out unpleasantries such as their parents' scoldings and corrective criticism. Sometimes they listen, sometimes they don't, and it's often hard to tell how much is sinking in.

But the main point is this: they *see* everything. They miss nothing. Their eager eyes, like their lithe little bodies, constantly flit around, roving and scanning, noticing every detail of their parents' lives. Children, it seems, are wired this way: to watch how adults, and most of all their parents, go about the business of living.

If what they see are manifestations of your own strengths of character—your sound judgment, responsibility, courageous perseverance, self-control, faith, hope, charity—they pay serious attention. They perceive confident, adult-level strength in you, and this awareness leads them to respect you. Children must, above all, respect their parents, and (we cannot stress this too much) all respect derives from perception of strength.

This respect, in turn, leads children to imitate their parents, to emulate their thinking and behavior, their attitudes and values. In this way, over the course of years children gradually, unconsciously internalize and adopt their parents' character.

In other words, you are teaching most about the virtues, indeed about yourself, when you scarcely realize it. Your snatches of conversation, your reactions to events (good and bad), your assessment of people and your dealings with them, your earnest personal prayer, your exertion in work and play, your comments on the news, your humor, whatever angers or delights you, even the look in your eyes: all these details sink into your children's minds and hearts. In fact, what children *overhear* at home is at least as important as what you say to them directly, often much more so.

So, please think about this . . .

Where, under what circumstances at home, do your children witness you living responsibly?

When do they see you stick with a task, refusing to quit?

How do they learn about your thoughtful judgment, your ethical principles? What sort of family conversation do they overhear at home—or is TV noise drowning you out?

Where and when do they see you exercise self-controlled moderation in food, drink, and entertainment?

When do they see and hear you pray at home, or anywhere else? Do they see you treat God as a *person* to whom we owe love, gratitude, and obedience?

Do they ever see you work, when your character strengths are on full throttle?

Do they see you practice courtesy (*please, thank you*, and actions that show these attitudes) toward your spouse and guests—and, indeed, toward them?

Do they see you happy from *doing* good, not just *feeling* good? Do they see how your acts of loving service (and theirs) lead to your satisfaction, peace, and joy?

Do they see and hear you express how grateful you are that you married your spouse, a person of great character?

Do they see you determined to struggle against your faults, to become a better person yourself—so that everyone in the family, not just the children, is moved by an active spiritual ideal?

In sum, parents cannot teach character effectively unless they first set example for their children. If you want to be a good parent, you must struggle first to be a good person.

Directed practice

Let's not forget, virtue is a habit of living rightly—and all habits are built by repeated practice. You, as a parent, must lead your children to *act*, to learn by doing.

A smart parent is savvy enough to grasp this rock-solid reality: Children are acquiring habits, whether good or bad, all the time.

Whatever children practice over and over again, whether virtue or vice, sets into concrete. If they're inert every day, they grow up lazy. If they wait for adults to clean up their messes, they'll never shift for themselves. If they're encouraged to read every day, they become readers. If they absorb large daily doses of TV, they become flabby couch potatoes and grow to esteem and imitate "celebrities." If they always get their way, they never learn self-control. If they say "please" and "thank you" often enough, they voice these words on their own; if not, they remain as rude ingrates. If they make their beds each morning, they turn this into a routine part of their daily ritual. If they redo slapdash homework each night, they learn to do it right the first time. And on and on.

Every single day, the children are forming permanent habits—the question for parents is, which ones?

This is where your real work comes in as a parent. This is where you make sacrificial effort every day, for years, to turn your children's daily habits into lifelong virtues.

You lead children to become responsible by directing them to live responsibly: to carry out their chores and do their homework to the best of their ability, to clean up their own messes, to live with the consequences of their neglect, to practice good manners in the family and outside the home, to tell the truth and keep their word.

You teach them justice by correcting their rudeness and selfish disregard for others' rights, especially with their siblings. You teach right from wrong by giving swift, just, consistent punishment for wrongdoing, and praise when they do right. You make them apologize.

You teach them fortitude by pressing them to persevere in a tough task, not to live as a quitter or whiner. You do not manage their affairs but rather *direct* them; that is, you do not do their work for them or micromanage their efforts. Instead, you show them what to do and then say, "Try it this way; you can do it on your own." You do not step in unless they've first given an earnest best effort; then you show them how the job is done and help them learn from mistakes. As someone wise once said, "Courage is the memory of past successes." In all this, you lead them to grow in confidence from putting their powers up against challenges. Their self-confidence grows from your confidence in them.

You teach healthy, realistic self-esteem from work well done, and so you engender in them a lifelong sense of professionalism, which is simply the virtues as lived in the workplace. If their work is messy and careless, you press them to do it over again, and then praise them when it's done right. You show them that work is for service, not vanity.

In short, you teach them an all-important lesson about life: comfort and convenience are only by-products of a successful life, not its purpose. We are here to serve others with our powers; that's what adult life is really all about. You lead them, through specific directed action, to forget about their self-centered interests, as you do, and contribute to the needs and welfare of the family. All this, you foresee as a parent, is practiced preparation for their later lives as husbands and wives, fathers and mothers, workers and citizens.

As a parent, you never give up until your children have acquired the powers to live rightly on their own.

One smart father told me his experience teaching his two daughters to pick up the mess in their rooms.

He said: "I kept telling my girls that they were old enough by now (ages nine and eleven) to keep their rooms clean, but the messes continued. Their habits of sloppiness from childhood remained unchanged, and this was driving my wife crazy.

"It occurred to me that my girls might not understand the starting-point concept of 'clean room,' so I decided to teach them myself. I set up what I called 'the ten-minute drill.' That is, I went into their room and picked up their things with them—the three of us together, working to finish the job in ten minutes. At the end, when everything was shipshape, I pointed around the room and said, 'This, girls, is a clean room. Understand?'

"This I did with them two or three nights a week for a couple of months. At one point, I told them to go do it on their own. By then they knew what I was talking about; I had shown them my standards for order. When I inspected their room, naturally I praised them for their work, told them I was proud of them, which pleased them a lot. I also showed them how little time it takes when we really set our minds to a job. Their work wasn't perfect every time thereafter, but we made serious progress."

(See Chapter 5 for details about how leadership and rules work in the family.)

Word

Finally, verbal explanation.

Many parents, it seems, believe that talks—lectures, scoldings, reprimands, and the like—are the main way of forming children's character. This belief is mistaken. Personal example and parent-directed practice are far more powerful. Talk in any form is most effective, maybe only effective, when it acts to explain or remind or encourage children about what they witness and are led to do in family life.

In other words, verbal explanation works mostly to form children's judgment and conscience—to give a rational understanding to the parents' ongoing example and their requirements for living the other virtues: responsibility, persevering toughness, self-control, and a spirit of generous forgiveness. Your explanations provide the *why*.

For instance, you and your spouse say "please" and "thank

you" to each other and insist that your children do the same. As often as necessary, you explain why: because other people have dignity, rights, and feelings, and these we're obligated to respect. (That is, the existence of other people's rights leads to our obligations.)

Another instance: You and your spouse put things back where they belong and you make your children do likewise. You explain that grown-ups dislike messes and no one should have to search for something mislaid through our self-centered carelessness. Others' needs take priority, always, over our own sloth and sloppiness.

Another: You and your spouse stick with a job around the house until it's done right, and you make the kids follow suit with their chores and homework. You explain the importance of work well done and the disgrace of being a slacker or quitter. In the grown-up world of work, everyone is routinely expected to turn out competent performance, and the best professionals consistently do high-quality work, whether they feel like it or not. This adult-level power takes years of practice, and it must begin in childhood.

Yet another example: You and your spouse refuse to watch programs that treat human beings as mere objects (the essence of "materialism"), and you won't allow such programs in your house. You explain your moral convictions and how you and your family strive to live by them. When your children are adults, you explain to them, they can direct their own families by light of their own convictions, which you hope will be the same as yours. But in the meantime, it's your home and therefore your decision about what's allowed and what's not—period.

The point here is that you rely on talk only to reinforce and explain action, to help the children grasp why you live the way you do and why you press them to do the same: "This is the way competent, responsible, considerate adults behave: the way you should live when you grow up as adolescents and adults. We, your parents, direct you and correct you because we love you."

As any parent who has grappled with life in the trenches will tell you, children roundly resist this lesson-giving. They will not understand, or will just heatedly refuse to understand, what you tell them. This resistance flares up especially during the two most troubled stages of children's lives: at ages two to five, and again at thirteen to seventeen. These are emotional ages of life, where strong feelings skew perception and mess up motivations. All the same, you and your spouse steel yourselves and patiently persevere. You live by the granite faith that someday, sooner or later, your children will finally understand. At some point, maybe years from now, they'll remember what you said, and your lessons will finally sink in, especially when they start their own families. (Hasn't this happened to you already? Don't you now fully grasp and appreciate, at last, your own parents' loving leadership and encouragement and corrections?)

What we must underscore here is that practice builds habits, while explanations—heart-to-heart talks, stories of heroism, strong corrections, scoldings, and the like—build judgment, conscience, attitudes, values. Talk alone can never replace parental example and purposeful practice. Rather it fortifies good habits, roots them in place for keeps, by explaining the reasons behind them.

So, conversation between parents and kids is hugely important, and this takes stretches of time. This is why the electronic media, the biggest thief of time in family life, must be kept under control. Parents need all the time they can get to talk with their growing children, especially in those crucial matters that will shape their consciences.

It seems to be a fact of life: *For most people, the voice of conscience is the voice of their parents—the memory of their parents' lessons about right and wrong.*

Your conversations with your children should lead them to understand the whole range of your judgment, values, convictions, and sense of family honor. You explain your family's history as best you know it: how the children's forebears were such strong, courageous people. (The generation who struggled through the Great Depression and World War II were truly heroic.) You tell them stories about your work, what you do for a living each day. (Since they probably don't see you on the job, you must tell them about it. If you fail to do this, how will they know?) You explain current events, your impressions of prominent figures in the news, and people past and present whom you respect, and why.

Children should grow to know their parents' thinking so well that they can predict how they'd react to almost anything.

Above all, you should listen. You learn so much from listening to your children: their progress in judgment and conscience, their worries and self-doubts, their problems. Children's problems seem small, even laughably trivial to adults, but they're big burdens to children. When you listen, you can better understand and explain and encourage.

If you listen to your children when they're small, they will be sincere with you when they're adolescents, and this is vitally important. At that most uncertain and fearful time of their lives, they will turn to you for guidance, lean on your strength, rely on your judgment, draw confidence from your love.

Please bear this in mind: Experience shows that adolescents who deeply love and respect their parents remain virtually immune to perilous peer-pressures and untouched by the rock-sex-drugs culture. Their parents' character is the measure by which they judge their peers.

One final and important thought here: When you chat with your children, be sure to *listen with your eyes.* Children are extremely sensitive to what they see in their parents' eyes. Make eye-contact with them to show your undivided attention; that's how important they are to you. When they look into your eyes, let them see your heartfelt love for them, your hopes for their future, your pride in their growing character.

ISSUES FOR REFLECTION AND DISCUSSION

(1) This chapter mentions several "invisible realities" that parents must lead their children to see and adopt: *honor, integrity, self-mastery, courage, courtesy, dedicated service, sacrificial love, conscience, God, grace, the soul.* What others would you add?

(2) Given the importance of example and repeated practice in forming a child's character, how have the following recent changes in family life acted to impede this dynamic? In other words, how have these developments interfered with child's growth in character as outlined here?

a. The home is mainly a place of leisure, not the workplace it was in former times. So children seldom, if ever, see their father work—or their mother, either, if she also works outside the home. They see their parents mostly relax, but they don't know what they're relaxing from. They see their parents as consumers, not producers.

b. Children's work at chores is no longer really needed at home. So kids have no outlet for their powers to contribute in small but appreciated ways to the family's welfare. Children, even older children and teens, spend most of their time at play.

c. Since almost nothing at home is handmade or fashioned from scratch, children have only a vague idea of the relationship between effort and results.

d. The electronic media have replaced conversation and reading as the ways by which kids learn about adult life.

e. Boys spend hours at computer games deriving pleasure from killing thousands of "virtual" people.

f. Entertainment figures—glamorously portrayed as powerful, aggressively self-assured, funny, successful, wildly adored by crowds—make many parents seem comparatively weak and dull. So when children naturally search for someone strong to imitate, they are drawn to media figures. They respect talk-show hosts and comedians more than their parents.

(3) In today's society, the right/wrong dichotomy has become a question of *age*—"For mature audiences only. . . . Under 17 not admitted." How can parents correct this at home?

(4) Comment on this statement: Children do not look for a set of propositions to live by. Rather, they silently ask themselves, "Who lives a great life? Whom do I want to be like?"

(5) A large part of the respect we have for people derives from their reputation; we tend to esteem people who are strongly esteemed by others. How can each parent enhance the other's "reputation" in the home? That is, what

can the father say and do at home to show the children his heartfelt esteem for his wife? And the wife for her husband?

CHAPTER TWO

More about the Virtues

We're still looking at the big picture of parents' vocation here, but now we want to sharpen the focus, see the virtues in clearer detail, make the job description and goals more specific.

What we're outlining in this chapter is a more detailed frame of reference. If you're like most parents today, you need a framework for seeing, and then smartly acting on, your children's progress toward maturity.

We've already mentioned this five-fold framework: sound judgment, a sense of responsibility, fortitude, self-mastery, and greatness of heart. For years I used this breakdown to counsel parents about their formative job, and many gratefully told me how much it helped them.

I want to spell out the framework's details here, somewhat in the abstract but still useful. Once you see these common-sense components (all interrelated, of course), you can act more effectively and confidently. The rest of the book will show how fathers and mothers work to build each of these virtues. But before we move into the how, we need to finish mapping out the why: What are we trying to accomplish here?

Veteran parents will tell you: If your *why* is strong enough and clear enough, you can figure out most of the *how* for yourself.

In family life, as in business or even war, if a strategy is clear and the goal passionately sought after, then you need not get bogged down worrying about tactics. A good strategy helps you better choose the most sensible courses of action. If you know what you are after, if you have a compass to keep you on track, you can afford to improvise, experiment, approach from different angles, try what other parents have done, and even make mistakes along the way. As long as you keep moving toward your objective—relentlessly, courageously, without giving up or letting up—you have a fighting chance of winning in the end.

A smart dad once explained his philosophy to me like this:

"When I was taking driving lessons a long time ago, my father gave me some good advice. He said that when a driver is approaching a tight squeeze—with only a foot or so of space on each side of the car—he should just aim ahead, look past the obstacle, and keep driving. He shouldn't be so overcautious as to slow to a crawl and fearfully glance back and forth between the sides, struggling to gauge the space in fractions of an inch. If you do this, he said, you might hit something or get bumped from behind because you're moving too slow. He said that as long as you look straight ahead and keep moving, then somehow, mysteriously, you'll pass safely on through.

"I've found that this works with being a parent, too. Don't get hung up and paralyzed by problems along the way. Just look ahead to your kids' future and keep heading there, no matter what. Somehow, mysteriously, it works; you bypass the obstacles and forge ahead. In parenting, as in driving, I think, it's confidence that keeps you going."

So here, one by one, are the strengths your children should have fixed like granite in their minds and wills and hearts before they leave your home for good.

Sound judgment

How can we understand the power of sound judgment, that is, thinking like a mature, responsible adult? Here are some ways of looking at it—ways that you can explain to your children:

• Fundamentally, sound judgment is the power of *discernment*. That is, it's the *acquired ability to make distinctions*, especially the great distinctions in life—truth from falsehood, good from evil, right from wrong. (More on this in Chapter 8.) On the moral plane—that is, in the interplay between rights and duties—it's our conscience.

Related to this, judgment is the power to understand human nature and life-experience: what is important in life from what is not, what is important in people and what is not. We have good judgment when we have the power to weigh people's motivations, values, and priorities in life. It is the power to recognize the good, the true, and the beautiful in life and in other people—and to distinguish these from the evil, the false, and the sordid.

Someone once asked an Oxford professor what he thought was the purpose of education. His answer: "Why, it's so young people can recognize rubbish when they see it!" Not a bad definition. As a result of their upbringing, at home and in school, young people should know lies, propaganda, and phoniness of all sorts when they see these things.

• Sound judgment is also *shrewdness*. It's the ability to appreciate the good in people, to grasp what moves them most in life: that is, their values and ideals. It's the power to size people up quickly and deeply, but without the desire to dominate them. Aristotle said (to paraphrase him) that a philosopher, someone who loves truth and goodness, combines shrewdness and good will. Someone who is both shrewd and good-willed has the essence of wisdom. Great parents have this kind of lynx-eyed, benevolent shrewdness, and their children learn from this wisdom.

• Sound judgment is *the ability to foresee the probable consequences, both good and bad, of a projected course of action*. Also of

35

inaction, for neglecting to act in time also has consequences, often disastrous. It's the power to make realistic risk-assessments. It involves learning from the mistakes and successes of ourselves and others. (For obvious reasons, teenagers' driver-education programs stress judgment as much as reflexive skills. Most teenagers' problems, not just behind the wheel but in other areas of life, arise from rickety judgment.)

• Sound judgment also means a respect for learning and intellectual achievement, that is, *culture.* This is a cordial familiarity with the greatest achievements of the human spirit, those accomplishments of mind, will, heart, and body that inspire us and prove that humans are not mere beasts. All great art, it is said, makes us proud to be human. And great literature leads us to see life through others' eyes; it expands our vision, deepens our judgment, and liberates us from the bonds of the *local,* the *present,* and the *self.*

• Conscience, the moral dimension of sound judgment, is the framework for judging the right thing to do in a tangled situation. It tells us what we *ought* to do so that we live ethically, honorably, in friendship with God and at peace with others, respecting their rights and dignity and feelings. This power of conscience is not just a bundle of shapeless sentiments; it's a thoughtful understanding of good and evil, right and wrong, built up through a lifetime of learning, but especially during the years of youth.

Responsibility

What is responsibility? The Greeks called it *justice* and said it meant giving others what is due to them. The word "duty" is related to "due"—a duty is something owed to others by right.

If any of the great virtues come naturally to children, it

would seem to be this one. Children call it "fairness," and they have a keen, powerful sense of what is fair. For this reason, you can usually correct kids effectively when you appeal to their sense of fairness: "It's unfair to your mother to leave your chores around the house undone; she shouldn't have to clean up messes you have made." Wise parents discover this early on, and so they put correction to the children in terms of what's fair. This lays a solid ground for more complex lessons of ethics later in the children's lives, especially during adolescence.

This virtue of responsibility is rich with meanings. Here is how you can explain it to your children:

• Responsibility means acting so as to respect the rights of others, including their right not to be offended. (So it overlaps with charity, that is, thoughtfulness for others' feelings.) *Because other people have rights, we have obligations.* My right to throw a punch stops short of someone else's face. I have a right to scribble a big drawing, but not to smear graffiti on someone's wall. I have a right to stand in line, but not to butt in. I have a right to shop, but not to have others foot the bill. I have a right to speak my mind, but not to interrupt or intentionally offend someone. The whole moral development of children is to move them from *self* to *others*.

• Responsibility is a *habit of doing our duties whether we feel like it or not.* In family life, it is sacrificial love. Love means shouldering and carrying out our family obligations: in family life, responsibility shows our love.

And in the world of work, responsibility means professionalism—the power to perform at our best no matter how we feel. Real professionals carry out their responsibilities, perform their services as best they can, even when they don't feel like it. Headaches, personal concerns, emotional ups and downs—none of these things deter effective professionals (or parents) from fulfilling their duties of service.

• Responsibility is *respect for rightful authority*. Authority means, among other things, the right to be obeyed. Great parents may be unsure about many things in their children's upbringing, but they have no doubts about their rightful authority. Successful parents are confident of their authority. They take for granted, so to speak, that their children will respect and obey them. As a result, their children, over time, grow to have *confidence in their parents' self-confidence*.

To look at it another way, effective fathers and mothers see their parenthood as a kind of high office, like that of president or Supreme Court justice. Whoever bears the burden of responsible public office, regardless of personal shortcomings, has a right to be respected and obeyed. So, too, no matter what personal faults or self-doubts they may have, parents, by the very fact of their parenthood, have a right to their children's respectful cooperation.

• Responsibility also means *living with the consequences of our decisions and mistakes, including our neglect.* (How many problems in our society derive from attempts to escape responsibility?) Responsible people do not shift blame; they refuse to see themselves as victims. They admit their mistakes honestly and shoulder the consequences.

• Responsibility is the *willingness and ability to honor our promises and commitments even when this involves hardship.* Responsible people will endure sacrifice to keep their word. Because their given word means much to them, they do not make promises quickly or carelessly.

• Responsibility is the *habit of minding our own business, staying out of matters that do not concern us.* Mature people do not snoop, gossip, or meddle. Consistently, they give people the benefit of the doubt, and they respect people's right to presumption of innocence. (Savvy bosses know that gossips tend to be slackers; those employees who meddle in everyone else's business usually neglect their own.)

Responsible children learn from their parents how to use their powers to contribute to family welfare. They receive encouragement as well as correction from their parents, and so they grow in confidence. In a real sense, *responsibility is another word for maturity.* Children become mature not when they reach puberty and grow in physical stature, but when they think and act consistently like other-centered adults.

You can explain it this way to your youngsters: *Responsibility means just this: if we don't do what we're supposed to do, somebody else gets hurt. We do our duty so that other people won't suffer.*

Fortitude

Fortitude is the third great virtue. We also know it by other names: *courage, perseverance, toughness, "guts."*

Outside of war or some physical threat to our safety (as in our poorest city neighborhoods), physical courage isn't often needed in civilized society. But moral courage certainly is. Moral life means taking risks and grappling with hardship— including the problem of looking different from our peers. Many young people never learned the concept while growing up, never knew firsthand any sort of adversity. For this, they and their families suffer.

You can explain fortitude this way to your children:

• Fortitude is the *acquired ability either to overcome or to endure difficulties: pain, discomfort, disappointment, setbacks, worry, tedium, looking "different."* It is the strength of will to either solve a given problem or just live with it—but in no case to seek irresponsible escape.

How many dreadful problems among teens and young married couples spring from a fixed, habitual resort to escape, from young people's low tolerance for hardship or even inconvenience? How is this weakness related to our problems with drugs and alcohol abuse, and so much of our staggering divorce rate?

• *Personal toughness is a habit of overcoming anxiety through purposeful, honorable action.* We turn our worries into action. It is the opposite of whining inertia in the face of problems, a compulsion to feckless complaint. Courageous people, in fact, see escapism—fleeing from inconvenience—as unworthy, even dishonorable.

Personal courage, enhanced by sound judgment, means coming to terms with a fact of reality: that life brings hardships, and many of these are unavoidable, even insoluble. But we adults learn to cope with them as best we can; we just put them behind us and get on with life. Related to this is the realistic understanding that, most of the time, expectation hurts more than reality: that is, anticipated problems nearly always seem worse than they turn out to be once we tackle them.

• To look at it another way, this strength is a *confidence in our problem-solving abilities, built through a lifetime of practice in solving problems.* Athletics, jobs around the house, schoolwork and homework, meeting deadlines, working at our best under reasonable pressure—all these build courage and self-confidence. So does steady, affirming encouragement from parents: "You can do it if you try"... "Stick with it and you can lick it"... "You're stronger than you think."

It seems to be a fact of life in youngsters' upbringing: Some reasonable adversity is healthy for children. There's such a thing as good stress. Outside of certain misguided schools, nobody in society "works at his own pace." If our forebears had worked at their own pace, we would still be riding in donkey carts and lighting our homes with candles. It took gutsy risk-taking and sustained hard work to produce all our wondrous labor-saving devices. When we're under reasonable stress and adversity, we all do our best work.

• Fortitude is also our *determination to overcome personal short-comings.* This means making the most of the good side of our natural temperament while working to overcome the downside. If we are shy, we learn to be a friendly, attentive listener, for a "good listener" usually attracts good friends. If we're impulsive, we learn to restrain ourselves from excess and foresee consequences; we then direct our zestful energy to achievement. If we are lazy, we strive toward purposeful action. If we fail to understand something, we seek advice from people we respect and otherwise think matters through. And so on.

In a sense, the power of fortitude is the exact opposite of "getting in touch with our feelings," a woefully common outlook today in too many schools and families. To be sure, sentiment has its place in life. Powerful emotions of love and loyalty, directed as they are to others' welfare, can move us to greatness. But in real life, self-centered feelings must give way to duty; if they do not, then young people have practically no capacity for *sacrifice*, which is the absolute essence of real love. Genuine love means *ignoring our self-centered feelings for the sake of others.* In grown-up life, love means serving others courageously. To be a great parent takes guts.

One example of heroic courage in family life is the way great parents persist relentlessly to teach good manners to their children. Dad and Mom say over and over again, hundreds of times: "Say *please* . . . , say *thank you* . . . , say *excuse me*. . . ." They keep at this patiently for months and even years until finally, miraculously, their children voice these terms on their own.

One mother told me how she saw this task: "It's like hammering a nail into a very hard wall, like cinder block. You keep tapping and tapping with the hammer, putting a little bit of pressure on the nail over and over again. For a while, sometimes a long while, you see no progress at all. Maybe you're moving a few molecules out of the way with each tap, but you don't see much to show for your effort. After a while, the nail starts to settle in. Eventually, after a long time, it's solidly in the wall—it's in for keeps, and you can hang anything from it.

"And that's the way it is with the kids. You teach *please* and *thank you* over and over again, even when you see no change, even when they keep falling back into habits of grabbing. You have faith that somehow, if you keep at this no matter what, sooner or later they'll get the message and change. Eventually, at last, they do just that—and the habit's in them for life."

Self-mastery

The fourth great virtue, *self-mastery*, or temperance, is one of the virtues we esteem most in people. In our self-indulgent culture, a temperate man or woman stands out from the crowd. Sometimes, especially in teen years, it takes courage to resist peer pressures and stand apart as one's own master.

Children grab for pleasures and power. They give free rein to their appetites and passions and doggedly resist the word "no." In a sense, they're often enslaved to their fears and feelings. If they grow up this way, they are headed for serious trouble.

No question about it, there's a lot riding on how well or how badly parents lead their children to control themselves, to curb their children's passions and cravings by artful use of the word "no." What does self-mastery mean? What should you teach your children about it, and its urgent importance?

• Temperance is power to say *no*, at will, to our laziness, passions, and appetites. It is the power, built up through practice, to *wait* for rewards and to *earn* them. A self-controlled man or woman, like everyone else, wants instant gratification, but does not expect it or need it. Self-controlled people do not turn wants into needs, and they know the difference.

Self-indulgent people grab for gratifications now and put off hard effort for later. Self-controlled people do just the opposite. They have a lifetime habit of earning what they want.

• Temperance means sensible enjoyment. Self-controlled people enjoy pleasures of life in moderation, never (or hardly ever) to excess. They don't go overboard in food, drink, entertainment, or even work itself. Because they are self-directed, they appear to others as quietly self-confident, on top of life. Their enjoyment comes from other people, not just things. To the extent that they take pleasure in food, drink, entertainment, and work, it's because of the company—family and friends—with whom they share these things. They are affable, fun to be with, enjoyable to work with. Their greatest delight is to delight their friends.

• Temperance means mastery of one's speech and actions. Self-controlled people do not use coarse language gratuitously. Only some rare, outrageous provocation prods them to cussing outburst, and they follow up with apologies when called for. They have a habit of controlling their speech, thus showing respect for the people around them.

• Temperance means mastery of one's time and affairs. Self-controlled people know how to manage time. In fact, the business catchword "time management" is just another name for self-control. Self-disciplined people know how to plan ahead, set their own deadlines, and stick to them. They neither exaggerate nor underestimate the size of a task and the time needed to complete it.

• Temperance means habitual courtesy. Self-disciplined people have a lifelong habit of saying and meaning *please, thank you, I'm sorry*, and *I give my word.* . . . If they offend anyone, even unintentionally, they are quick to apologize. They extend courtesy to everyone, and they can do this even in the face of rudeness or provocation.

In a word, temperate people have "class." Their character is marked by self-restraint, etiquette, healthy self-respect, an active spirit of service, an ongoing and active concern for the dignity and needs of those around them. To everyone who knows them, they are esteemed as great friends.

Habitual self-control does more than give grace to our lives. It's also vital to physical safety. Adolescents who have never acquired self-control—and who are thus driven by thoughtless impulse—can kill or cripple themselves, along with their friends.

Consider this. In the fall of 1995, the U.S. Government released results of a ten-year study on the causes of teenage automobile fatalities. Results were surprising: only 5 percent of these fatal accidents were caused by drunk driving. (For adult car fatalities, the figure is almost 50 percent.)

So, what caused 95 percent of these deaths among teens? You can guess. Speeding, showing off, road rage, reckless driving, ignoring stop signs and other warnings, and general inexperience. In other words, nearly all these young people were killed through uncontrolled impulsiveness, irresponsibility, or poor judgment.

The power of self-mastery prevents tragedies. It saves lives.

Heart

Last in our list is *greatness of heart.* This is the all-important spiritual power that gives force to all the other virtues. It directs our powers of judgment, responsibility, toughness, and self-control toward the well-being of other people, starting with our family and radiating out to friends, colleagues, acquaintances, strangers, our country.

The ancient Romans called it *magnanimity,* "greatness of soul." In our Judeo-Christian tradition, it goes by other names: *charity, compassionate understanding, awareness of others' needs, a spirit of service, sacrificial love.*

It is the capacity and desire to surpass ourselves, to endure or overcome anything for the sake of somebody else's welfare and happiness. It's *generosity*—the drive to give others the best of what we have for their sake, and expect little or nothing in return.

Consider this virtue in terms of your children's future values, and look at it like this: Where does someone put his heart? What does he love most in life? What would he be willing to suffer for, even die for? Answer these questions and you put your finger on that person's values.

This word "values" has swirled in a lot of controversy lately. It has cropped up in heated political wrangles over classroom curricula and media censorship. We want here to stay clear of these public-policy thickets and look at values as they're taught at home.

The fact is, everyone has values. Everyone holds something closest to his heart and leaves other things at a distance.

To speak of people's values, therefore, is to speak of their *priorities* in life: what comes first to them, then what comes second, third, and on down the line. Where, in what order, do people put their passions? What do they love most?

So, people differ in their values because they differ in what they love most and least. Look at this list of things that people love and live for—what they passionately pursue as the object of their heart:

- God
- family and friends
- country
- money
- truth
- fame and glory
- satisfying, service-oriented work
- career advancement
- comfort and convenience
- addictive substances
- pleasure and amusement
- power over others
- safety and security
- conformity: acceptance by others, being fashionably "with it"
- vengeance

Please teach this lesson to your children: We can tell people's values by which of these loves they hold closest, and which they belittle or ignore.

Some parents give their hearts to God, family, friends, truth, and service-directed work. Everyone who knows these parents, including their children, considers them great people. When children love and respect their parents, they grow to internalize their same loves and in the same order; that is, they adopt their parents' values.

Other parents, unfortunately, put power, career, and comfort ahead of anything else, and their families suffer, both now and later. Self-absorbed parents, it seems, form self-absorbed children.

In adolescence, teens are strongly tempted to put conformity and pleasure ahead of their family. But if Mom and Dad won their hearts in childhood, that is, if teenagers' love for family comes first, they can shunt these allurements aside. They love their parents deeply, and so will never betray them. At least not for long, not permanently.

So then, do your children know your priorities, the loves you hold above all others? Tell them. Urge them to follow you, to embrace your values as their own and live by them. And warn them about one of life's greatest disasters: to marry someone with mismatched priorities—whose values conflict with their own.

Up to now, we've been studying what we have to impart to children. But here, in the question of heart, we also have much to learn from children.

In the third century B.C., the Chinese philosopher Mencius said, "A great person is one who never loses the heart he had as a child."

It's obvious (once we see it) that the great character strengths have to be formed from scratch in children as they grow up, for kids do not enter the world with judgment, responsibility, courage, or self-control. Nonetheless, children do have beautiful qualities that must survive intact throughout childhood and into later life.

It's true, parents must patiently lead their children to become adults who are competent, learned, tough-minded, responsible, shrewd and savvy, nobody's fool. But, at the same time, as they grow up, children should never lose the great loves that they had as small children, loves they see still alive and growing in you.

What are these great loves of childhood?

• *Love for God.* Once they've been taught religious faith by their parents, children have a humble, sincere, and beautiful trust in God, whom they see as an all-powerful, all-loving Father.

As adults, great people never lose this vision and faith of childhood. They see themselves as children of God all their lives, watched over by the Creator's loving protection. This hope-filled confidence empowers them to withstand any hardship in life and steels them with a stalwart sense of responsibility, ethical uprightness, a clean conscience, what the Scriptures call "righteousness." God lives in the home, not just in church.

• *Love for family.* Tiny children have a natural and abiding affection for parents and brothers and sisters, who are the compass of their young hearts, the center of their existence.

All their lives, adults should hold onto their loving trust in Dad and Mom, loyalty to their grown brothers and sisters, and wholehearted devotion to the families they form themselves. As in childhood, their families form the center of their lives.

• *Love for life, friends, laughter.* Children arise each morning seeing the day as an adventure, a call to delight and achievement with family and friends. With their loved ones they share the gift of laughter, that splendid sign of a light, clean heart.

So, too, as adults they should be moved by that same vision of life as adventure, enjoying each day as a gift, delighting in the companionship of friends. They should take their responsibilities seriously, but not themselves.

• *Love for those in need.* At their best, youngsters have an exquisite quality of mercy, a capacity for compassion. We see this in their tender care for a wounded little animal, or their heartfelt sympathy for a grieving friend. This capacity for mercy, feeling sorry for someone, must never be snuffed out.

All their lives, great men and women show mercy to others, extend their hearts and help to people in trouble. They hate sin but love the sinner. They strive for peace, forgive injuries, bear no ill will or grudges toward anyone. They know that charity does not mean donating old clothes; it means mostly compassionate understanding.

• *Love for the truth.* Tiny children, it seems, are naturally truthful; they are laughably inept when they first try to lie. They have a way of putting their little fingers right on the truth, often with startling insight, like the candid little boy in "The Emperor's New Clothes." Instinctively and with astonishing accuracy, they can judge people's character.

So also, in adulthood, they should shun all forms of phoniness; they should know malarkey when they see it. They should have the guts to tell the truth, admit when they're wrong, and apologize. They should never enslave themselves to the worst lie of all: self-deception. They should know who they are and what they stand for: lessons learned from Dad and Mom.

Great people, then, are those who possess within their souls the powers of adults and the hearts of children. Generously, they direct their lives to the needs of others, and they have the inner strengths to serve people effectively, starting with their families. To all who know them, they are "wise as serpents, innocent as doves"—great men and women.

Your job as a parent, your mission in life, is to raise your children to this ideal: to form generosity and character so deeply within them as to direct the course of their lives to greatness. This is what a great parent does.

ISSUES FOR REFLECTION AND DISCUSSION

(1) In this chapter, it's said that responsibility means doing what needs to be done so that others won't suffer, and so "responsibility" is another word for love. Yet children have trouble seeing and appreciating, on their own, how responsible their parents are. How can each parent, then, point out to children how the other spouse lives responsibly—and thus loves and serves the family?

(2) It's said that the happiest people we meet in life are those who somehow enjoy (or grow to enjoy) what they have to do anyway; that is, their duties. They find enjoyment in work as well as in leisure. How can parents convey this to their children? How does the artful use of sincere praise help children grow in this way?

(3) Concerning the list of values at the end of this chapter: What other values could you add to the list? How could this list be used as a framework for assessing characters in fiction, history, and biography (including your children's reading)? Movies and television dramas? Real-life people? But if done with real-life people, why should this be done with tact and charity, "hating the sin, loving the sinner"?

(4) An old adage says: "Tell someone he's brave and you make him brave." How does this pertain to forming children's risk-taking courage? How can parents teach their children that courage doesn't mean fearlessness; it means doing what's right *despite* our fears? Courageous people don't lose their fears; they just overcome them.

(5) It's said that we can change people's character but not their temperament. How can we distinguish these? That is, how can parents accept what can't be changed in their children while working to change what can? For instance, shy children are both quiet and fearful, but they can grow up to be quietly confident; they retain the natural quietness but lose the fear. Impulsive children are both energetic and thoughtless, but they can grow up to be thoughtfully energetic; they keep the zest but learn to foresee consequences. Some children are ruthlessly competitive, but they can grow up as sportsmanlike competitors; they keep the competitiveness but temper it with respect for others. Why is it important, then, for parents to think about and cultivate what's *good* in their children's temperament, even though this is entangled with flaws that need changing?

(6) People who are most successful in business and professional life seem to have two personal traits: a) they know how to concentrate and work hard at will, even when they don't feel like it; and b) they have excellent social skills; they are courteous, gracious, ethical, consistently good listeners and explainers. How do these traits relate to this chapter's discussion of the virtues? In what sense does the term "professionalism" mean living the virtues in the workplace? That is, how do competent professionals show strong character in their work: sound judgment, responsibility, perseverance, self-discipline, and consideration for others? And what effect does it have on children that they practically never see their parents (at least their father) work this way?

CHAPTER THREE

The Consumerist Family: Kids in Trouble

Before we move on to see how parents succeed with their children's upbringing, it would help to pause here and take a look at the opposite situation: those homes (and they are many) where parents somehow fail to form character in their children, where children grow older without really growing up and then later collide with trouble. Negative lessons are valuable. We can understand a job more readily, including the job of parenthood, by studying what happens when it's not done right, or not done at all.

Kids in trouble

Clearly, something is wrong in today's society. For some reasons, large numbers of parents are failing to form character in their children.

We look around in our workplaces and neighborhoods and see young people in their twenties who are immature and irresolute, soft and irresponsible, uneasy about themselves and their futures. They may be technically skilled in some field and hold down decently paying jobs, but their personal lives and marriages are a wreck. In their conduct and attitudes, they seem permanently stuck in adolescence, that dangerous mixture of adult powers and childlike irresponsibility. Some are crippled or destroyed by substance abuse. But even if they remain drug-free (what a strange term!), many see their professional work as mere ego gratification or (an adolescent attitude) just drudgery endured for the sake of "spending money." Great numbers of them live as heartless narcissists, caring little or nothing about their parents or their children, if they choose to have any. They retain within themselves, sometimes tragically, the flawed attitudes of childhood. For some reason, they never quite grew up.

It's clear, of course, that many young people like this were wounded, maybe permanently, by a childhood spent in dysfunctional families: drug and alcohol dependency, physical and sexual abuse, hopeless poverty.

But what is striking today, and more to our point here, is the huge percentage of seriously troubled youths from *normal* families. It seems that, in our society, the distinction between normal and dysfunctional has blurred. Or, to put it another way, some sort of subtle dysfunction is corroding large numbers of typical, middle-class homes.

We see this the results of this all around us. Children today grow up in busy families where father and mother live together, life is comfortable and physically secure, everyone enjoys the bountiful pleasures of a prosperous suburban lifestyle. Yet later on, in adolescence and young adulthood, their lives are ravaged by alcohol and other drugs, grievous and ongoing marital discord, feckless irresponsibility, lack of ideals or even goals in life, professional aimlessness and instability, reckless pleasure pursuit, trouble with the law, shapeless self-doubt and self-loathing, even murder and suicide.

Consider this disturbing fact: The suicide rate among young people in the United States is directly proportional to family income. It is kids from our wealthy and middle-income suburbs, not our poorest inner-city neighborhoods, who most often take their own lives.

What is going wrong in our supposedly normal middle-class families today that could account for these problems? What is happening at home—or not happening—such that children grow older without growing up, that they arrive at adulthood without enough judgment and will and conscience to set their lives straight?

Let's approach the problem this way:

Normal American families seem to fall into two broad categories. One we could call the self-absorbed *consumerist* family; the second is the other-centered *sporting adventure* family.

In the self-absorbed family, parents do not set out, on purpose, to form character in their children. They treat family life like a picnic, a passive pleasure-centered experience, and their kids often meet with later trouble. In the other-centered family, by contrast, parents do set out to form character. As a result, their family life becomes an ideal-driven adventure, a great sport, and their kids largely turn out well. Why is this so?

Let's look at the self-absorbed family first. In the following chapters, we'll contrast it with life in the sporting adventure family—where things, it seems, are done right, where the parents direct themselves with a compass, where character is imparted for life.

Consumerist parents are self-absorbed and unconcerned with growth in virtue, whether for themselves or their children. So they make family life mostly a steady series of pleasant diversions. Life for parents and kids centers around leisurely enjoyment, fun-filled entertainment—a seamless array of sports, abundant food and drink, TV shows, computer games, movies, music, parties, shopping.

Boredom, it seems, is the consumerist family's enemy, the nemesis to be shunned at all costs. So children in families like this are kept relentlessly busy, constantly amused. The parents' rules, if any, aim at damage control: keeping squabbles and hassles to a minimum, keeping the kids out of trouble, keeping the kids from wrecking the place.

In consumerist homes, therefore, children are steadily apprenticed through childhood as consumers, not producers. Every day, they avidly practice living as self-absorbed enjoyers and shoppers. Not surprisingly, youngsters from such picnic-like homes see life as mostly play, a lifetime entitlement to happy amusement. The life of grown-up work (as they dimly understand it) is solely for piling up "spending money"—we work in order to spend, we produce in order to consume. Who can blame them for this life-outlook? After all, this is all they experience in family life; and, as we've seen, children learn mostly from example and repeated experience.

Sooner or later, of course, any picnic dwindles down into boredom; people get up and amble on to more alluring diversions. And the same happens in the picnic-like consumerist family. Starting in their middle-school years, very many self-absorbed kids grow bored with juvenile amusements and avidly turn to novel kinds of powerfully pleasurable sensations: alcohol, drugs, the erotic and increasingly violent rock culture, vandalism, reckless driving, recreational sex. Kids raised to see life as play will treat the automobile as a toy, and so will be prone to kill or cripple. Because their life has centered on things, they're disposed to put things ahead of people, to treat people as objects, mere tools and toys for their use or amusement. Related to this, they see sex as a toy, a high-powered form of recreation, and so fall headlong into promiscuity, cohabitational "relationships," unwanted pregnancies, abortions, and disastrous marriages. This is no exaggeration. It happens literally every day.

The consumerist family: a composite picture

It's worth our while here to look more closely at the consumerist family's typical traits. What follows below is a composite picture of those unfortunate normal homes where children are poised for later trouble. That is, if you looked back to the childhood of many troubled adolescents and young adults, as described above, what traits of their family lives would you see over and over again with striking regularity?

Even with plenty of variations in detail, this is the pattern of consumerist families. Let's look at the parents first, then at the children.

Parents headed for trouble

Consumerist parents live divided lives. They live as producers at work but consumers at home. In fact, to their children they seem to work only in order to consume. Their home, far removed as it is from the real-life world of responsible adult achievement and ethical interpersonal dealings, is a place arrayed with entertainment gadgets, a site devoted to comfort, relaxation, and amusement. But this universe of comfortable delight is all that their children see—and for children, "seeing is believing." This cocoon of pleasant escapism wholly envelopes children and shapes their sole experience with life. It becomes the ambiance within which they fashion their deepest attitudes and habits, indeed their whole outlook on life: "Life is all about pleasure."

Being self-absorbed and centered mainly on the present, consumerist parents seldom think about their children's futures—that is, what sort of men and women their children will grow up to become. Their time horizon stretches, at most, only a few months or couple of years ahead. Almost never do they picture their children as grown men and women in their late twenties with job and family responsibilities of their own. When the parents do think of their kids' futures, they think in terms of career, not character. They think of what their children will *do*, not what they will *be*.

The parents seem to expect—in fact, utterly take for

granted—that their children will naturally grow up OK as long as they're kept busily amused and shielded (more or less) from outside influences. In other words, they think that adult-level ethics, conscience, and sound judgment will just gradually form in their children in a natural and unaided way, along with the children's physical stature. When the parents think of character at all, they think it's something to be *maintained* in children, not *formed from scratch*.

The parents come down to the children's level, as indeed all parents should—but (and here's the point) they *stay* there. By their own evident devotion to a "hassle-free" existence at home, off the job, they neglect to raise their children to grown-up levels of responsible thinking and acting. They do little to prepare the children for later life and lead them toward responsible service. Indeed, their children seem to have no concept what "adulthood" means—except for what they see in movies and TV dramas. The parents seem clueless that they have a job to do, an action to take, a change to make in their children's minds, hearts, and wills: to strengthen each child's conscience and character for life.

Both parents give in readily to children's wishes and "feelings," even when they judge that this might be a mistake. Very often in family life they permit what they disapprove of; that is, they let children's pleas and whining override their parental misgivings. The parents are moved by their children's smiles, not their welfare; they will give in on many issues to avoid a confrontational "scene."

Unwittingly, through their example of giving in, these parents teach their children to let strong desires, or even whims, routinely override judgments of conscience. So the children fail to distinguish between wants and needs; to the children, wants *are* needs. As a result, "feelings," not conscience, become a guide for action. (So, what happens later when the kids are tempted by the powerfully pleasurable sensations of drugs, alcohol, promiscuous sex? What is there to hold them back?)

The father is a weak moral figure in the home. He does not teach right from wrong in a confident, purposeful way, and he does nothing to prepare his older children for their later lives outside the home, especially in moral matters. He defers "children's things" to his wife. To his kids, he appears mostly as an amiable, somewhat dull figure, even a sort of older sibling. In family life, the kids see him wrapped up entirely in his own leisure activities (watching TV or playing sports) and minor repairs. Since they never see him work, they have no idea how he earns his living, or even what this term means. Moreover, he seldom shows much outward respect and gratitude toward his wife—so she, too, seems a weak figure to the children.

Parents are minimal in the practice of religion. Though the family may attend a house of worship from time to time, even regularly, this is done as thoughtless social routine. Family life includes little or no prayer, not before meals or at any other time. So children never witness their parents living a sense of responsibility toward God or some strong internalized ethic. "God" is just a word (sometimes an expletive), not a person, certainly not a friend. In the children's eyes, parents do not seem answerable to anyone or anything, except a relentlessly busy calendar.

Parents watch television indiscriminately, and they allow "adult entertainment" into the home. Though they may restrict, more or less, their children's access to inappropriate material, they are driving home a powerful message: "When you're old enough, anything goes."

Consequently, to the children, the right-wrong dichotomy becomes strictly a matter of age: "Whatever's wrong for kids is OK for grown-ups, so just wait till I turn fourteen!"

Children Headed for Trouble

At first glance most children from homes like this don't seem seriously troubled at all. Typically they're cheery and well-scrubbed, pleasant and smiling, often very active, but only for things they enjoy. They're habituated to pleasant sensations. They like to be liked, and in fact they expect to be liked no matter what they do. Since they're used to treating adults (including their parents) as equals, they appear naïvely lacking in respectful good manners. With some troubled exceptions here and there, they seem entirely carefree. Indeed most of them really are carefree, for now.

Children have a low tolerance for discomfort or even inconvenience. They are horrified by physical pain, however slight, or even the threat of it. They successfully plead and badger and stall their way out of unpleasant commitments and "hassles"—promises and previous agreements, music lessons, homework, chores, appointments, deadlines.

Children believe that just about anything may be done for a laugh. If a prank or ridiculing remark amuses them and their peers, they blithely indulge in it no matter who gets hurt. They think their entitlement to fun must shove aside other people's rights and feelings. Indeed, the existence of other people's rights and feelings almost never enters their minds. Their outlook on life remains unchanged from infancy: "Me first!"

Children enjoy an abundance of spending money and leisure time. As a fixed habit, they overindulge in soft drinks, sweets, and junk food. They spend countless hours wholly absorbed in electronic sensations (computer games, television, the Internet) and other types of amusement. They are generally free to consume whatever they want whenever they want it, and this they do.

Kids show little or no respect for people outside the family: guests, friends of parents, teachers, salespeople, the elderly. They seldom, if ever, display good manners in public. *Please* and *thank you* are missing from their speech. On birthdays or holidays, children rip through a mound of presents, but they neglect to write or call to say "thank you" to relatives—and see no reason to. In some instances, children might be superficially pleasant to people (as long as this costs them nothing), but they have zero concern for others' needs or interests.

Ironically, for all the parents' efforts to provide a pleasant home, the children hold little or no respect for them. The kids view their parents as "nice," and they'll admit they "like" Mom and Dad most of the time. But they simply do not esteem their parents as strong, and therefore emulatable, people. When asked whom they do admire, they rattle off a long list of entertainment figures, especially comedians and rock performers.

Children know next to nothing about their parents' personal histories, and nothing at all about grandparents and forebears. So they have no sense of family history and moral continuity, that is, how they are the latest in a long line of mutually loving people who struggled, often heroically, to serve each other and stick together through good times and bad.

The children have no heroes in their lives, no real people or historical or literary figures who surpassed themselves in service to others and, by fulfilling duties, accomplished great deeds. In the absence of heroes, the kids admire and pattern themselves after coarsely freakish media "celebrities" and make-believe cartoonish figures. (As someone said, "If kids have no heroes, they'll follow after clowns.")

Children don't care about causing embarrassment to the family. Often they don't even understand what that might mean, for they have no framework for grasping what's shameful. They are unmoved by any cultivated sense of "family honor." If children's dress and public behavior cause shame to the parents, that's just too bad.

Children complain and whine about situations that can't be helped: bad weather, reasonable delays, physical discomfort, moderately heavy workloads, personality differences, and the like. Their most common word of complaint is "boring." Since their lives at home are micromanaged rather than directed, they're accustomed to having their problems solved by oversolicitous grown-ups. They've found through experience that if they hold out long enough, someone will eventually step in to make their troubles go away. Consequently, they learn to escape problems, not solve them; they learn to shun discomfort, not endure it.

Children have no serious hobbies except television watching, computer games, and listening to music (mostly rhythmic noise). Their lives seem entirely plugged in to electronic devices, and they don't know what to do without them. Their thinking is dominated by the entertainment culture; in some senses, they *believe* in it. They know the words to dozens of songs and commercials, but they know nothing of the Ten Commandments.

Children (even older ones and teens) tend to form opinions by impulse and vague impressions. They are scarcely ever pressed to rely on reasons and factual evidence for their judgments. Thus they're easily swayed by flattery, emotional appeals, and peer-group pressures. They fail to recognize claptrap—as in advertising, pop culture, and politics—when they see it. They follow the crowd wherever it goes. They loosely sense that something is "cool," but they cannot express why.

Children never ask the question "Why?" except to defy directions from rightful authority. They are intellectually dull, even inert, showing little curiosity about life outside their family-school-playground universe. In school, moreover, they're often incorrigibly poor spellers and sloppy writers. That is, they are careless in work and do not take correction seriously. For them, nearly all enjoyment comes from escapist amusement, not from work well done, serious accomplishment, fulfillment of duty, serving others, or personal goals achieved through purposeful effort. If a task isn't "fun," they're not interested.

Children have little sense of time. Since they hardly ever have to wait for something they want, much less earn it, they have unrealistic expectations about the time needed to complete a task. They estimate either too much or too little. Consequently, large tasks are put off too long or small jobs appear mountainous. Even older children approaching high-school age have virtually no concept of deadline or of working steadily within a self-imposed time frame. The children seem to drift along in a free-floating, ever-present *now*—and this state of mind continues well into adolescence and even young adulthood.

Throughout high school and college, they view school as one last fling at life, not a preparation for it. Graduation looms as a poignantly sad event, for they see the best part of life as behind them, not ahead. What lies ahead is trouble—the "hassles" (as they put it) of real-life work, responsible commitments, day-to-day routine, budgets and bills, two-week vacations, sharply diminished freedom, and a steep decline in their standard of living. So who looks forward to this? Who can endure it? Why grow up?

As explained already, this picture of a family headed for trouble is just a composite sketch, not a comprehensive description. Certainly there are gradations among families; some families will show some of these characteristics, but not all of them. Nonetheless, over and over again, the features listed here show up in the personal histories of troubled adolescents and young adults who have come—we must stress this again—from apparently normal homes.

Materialism

Please consider whether you agree with this:

It's arguable that the young people described above are being steadily formed in the life-outlook of materialism.

This life-outlook does not mean, as many believe, merely the ambitious pursuit of things: fashionable clothes and cars, trendy expensive gadgets, a hefty portfolio. This sort of consumerist lust is only part of the problem. For after all, and as we've all experienced, many well-off people can possess all sorts of things without being materialistic.

Materialism really means *seeing and treating other people as things*. Materialism considers man (in the philosophical sense) as merely an object, a clever beast. This is where the evil lies.

The life-outlook of materialism has corollaries that directly affect the way people live and treat other human beings:

- Life ends with death; so there's no reward or punishment in any afterlife.
- We answer to no Higher Power for the way we live; we answer only to the law, if it can catch us.
- We can do anything we want to anyone, as long as it's legal.
- Conscience is just a bundle of sentiments.
- Morality is merely social convention.
- "Rights" are nothing but disguised interests and rationalized power-grabbing.
- Since people are just objects, then whatever things we want—money, possessions, fame, power—can come ahead of people.

- Work is for money, and money is for power and a pleasurable life.
- People are valued only for their usefulness or amusement, and can therefore be (legally) mistreated or discarded to suit our purposes.
- The only real evil is pain.
- Life has no purpose but the pursuit of pleasure and power.

This heartless and godless outlook on life—the belief that man is a beast—is the exact antithesis of Judeo-Christian morality, indeed of elementary decency among people of good will. Yet we find it promoted aggressively in business and professional affairs, in elements of the media, and in public life. We even find it, as we've seen above, seeping its way like acid into family life.

In a sense, this materialistic outlook comes from growing up without internalizing those significant invisible realities we mentioned before: God, the soul, honor, integrity, courage, conscience, and the rest. Young people who internalize nothing about the spiritual dimension of life will entrap themselves wholly in the material. Their life will center on themselves and their senses, their ego and their possessions. They'll never progress from serving self to serving others.

In the self-absorbed consumerist family, the enemy is boredom. In the sporting-adventure family, where parents work to build conscience and character, the real enemy is materialism. So, how do parents lead their children to shun materialism and live rightly? This is explained in the chapters that follow.

ISSUES FOR REFLECTION AND DISCUSSION

(1) Given that respect for people nearly always derives from some perception of strength, why do children from con-

sumerist families generally have little real respect for their parents?

(2) Please comment on this statement: For a family where boredom is the enemy, time is a problem; but for the healthy formative family—where there's a job to be done—time is a resource.

(3) It's a commonplace that too much of most things is un-healthy for children: too much ice cream, homework, television, leisure time, involvement with sports and extra-curriculars. Excess in most areas, it seems, causes dis-torted development. The question here: Is there such a thing as too much attention? How can children be dam-aged later (in marriage, for instance) by being brought up always in the limelight, always the center of parents' attention?

(4) Please comment on this: In former times, people worked hard all their lives to enjoy certain rewards in their later years. They looked forward to the payback for their life-time investment of work and risk-taking: leisure time, plenty of money, abundant food and drink, access to a wide array of sports and amusements, a powerful car, a house full of convenient labor-saving devices.

But today's middle-class children enjoy all these per-quisites from infancy, long before they've even begun to work. They enjoy, right now, everything that former gen-erations used to work toward, and look forward to, all their lives.

If anything, young people approaching their first job face a much harder life, one for which (if they grew up in picnic families) they've been ill-prepared. They lacked example of confident adults enjoying life even while cop-ing with challenges. They face tightened budgets, far less freedom, more work and responsibility, much less leisure time, a drop in their standard of living. Wistfully, they look back on childhood and adolescence as their "golden age." And so, like Peter Pan, they grasp tightly onto the delights of childhood and shrink back from growing up.

How does this state of affairs account for what we see among people in their twenties and thirties: a) long "relationships" without marriage, b) refusal to have children, c) grim overwork combined with obsession for amusement, d) reluctance to form commitments, e) suicide.

(5) Experience shows that many well-off middle-class, even wealthy, families are not materialistic. That is, even though they enjoy money and material possessions, neither the parents nor the children live like materialists: they do not treat people as things. Even if they lost all their money, we suspect, their lives would not be radically altered. Their lifestyles, yes, but not their relations with God and each other. How can we account for this?

(6) Please focus on a few of the traits of children from consumerist families as mentioned above and project their lives into the future. If these children's attitudes and conduct remain unchanged from what's described here, what sort of problems will they likely meet with later in their a) marriages and b) careers?

CHAPTER FOUR

Parent Leaders

Let's turn now to look at the healthy family—what we've called the *sporting adventure* family—where children's character is formed for life.

Invariably, parents in homes like this are busy. Like other fathers and mothers today, including those in the self-absorbed consumerist family, they struggle with bills and deadlines, schedules and problems and emergencies, the roller-coaster ups and downs of family life. But all these sacrificial efforts are focused, not wasted, because of the parents' vision—the compass that directs all they do.

Here's their secret. These effective fathers and mothers look far into the future, twenty or more years ahead, and picture their children as grown men and women, competent adults coping with family and career responsibilities of their own. That is, *they see their children as adults-in-the-making.*

Consequently, these far-seeing parents grasp that they have a job to do, a duty to carry out with their kids. They realize they have to work serious changes in their children, starting now, to build inner strengths that their kids presently and conspicuously lack. They have a goal to strive toward, as in a vigorous sport—that is, what kind of men and women their kids should grow to be. The family has plenty of fun, to be sure, as in any hard-fought athletic contest; but this delight comes from work as much as leisure, from accomplishing something important, a distant ideal that's worth today's sacrificial efforts.

In other words, these parents foresee that they have to civilize their children, to impart in them a lifelong conscience and character that will lead to their kids' later success in all aspects of life, but especially in marriage. This challenge is, in their eyes, what their parenthood is all about.

So, in the sporting adventure family, the parents struggle to live like responsible adults themselves, and they expect their children—lead their children—to do the same. Family rules are set in place not to control the children but rather to direct them. The rules have a purpose: to strengthen the kids' conscience and character through example and directed practice in responsible living. Family life is active, dynamic, as in any sport, and parents know all the triumphs and reverses, the temporary setbacks and disappointments, all the up and down struggles along the way until final victory—when their children emerge into adult life as confident, competent, responsible men and women.

Parents who want to turn their family life into an adventure must be smart enough to grasp this fact of life: *Parents either pay now, or they pay later.*

That is, parents who neglect their children's character upbringing, who take it easy now in a self-absorbed life, can pay an enormous price later when their children fall headlong into trouble.

But those fathers and mothers who sacrifice now to empower their children's characters can enjoy life later, when their children grow up to their high expectations: Their children will do the right thing without being told. Their children will tend to choose good friends and good dating partners and, later, a good spouse. Before they are out of their teens, the children will, with God's help, think and act like responsible adults, earn the respect of all who know them, and bring honor to their family.

Responsible parents act as leaders in the family. What does this mean?

Any time people engage in an important, responsible undertaking for others' welfare—whether a business, a job, government affairs, or a family—there's a need for clear, competent leadership. The more serious the challenge, the greater the need for someone to direct everyone's efforts in an inspiring, encouraging way toward the ultimate goal. (Note that a picnic-like family doesn't really need a leader, for it has no really serious goal. Where does a picnic lead?)

The real goal for the family, as we've seen, is to raise the children toward responsible adulthood. All the dynamics of family life lead to this: what kind of men and women the children will grow to be. No challenge is more important than this, and so great parents emerge in family life as real leaders.

How do they do this? How do fathers and mothers lead their children effectively? To form a picture of parental leadership, let's look at the characteristics of all sorts of leaders and see how parents fit the profile of leadership in family life.

Leaders are moved by a long-term vision, and so they win people's respect

Here's a broad statement that you'll probably agree with: in business and professional life and in affairs of state, our most respected leaders are those who look farthest toward the future and foresee oncoming perils and opportunities. Respected leadership and strategic foresight seem to go hand in hand. The farther and clearer the vision, the greater the respect.

If we page through the works of outstanding American leaders of the past—people such as George Washington, John Adams, Thomas Jefferson, Abraham Lincoln, Theodore Roosevelt, Martin Luther King—we are struck by their hopeful, future-directed vision. Frequently these leaders spoke of "posterity" and foresaw future events in a way that was both realistic and hopeful, an idealism without illusions.

In our own time, too, outstanding professional and business leaders have a clear long-term vision about their company's future success, and they communicate this goal, at least occasionally, to everyone who works with them. They think five to twenty years ahead, and this goal-setting drives them and their team forward, for they know that people's efforts are most effective when they're focused on some future achievement.

This dynamic seems to work in successful families, too. Parents, all kinds of men and women with different temperaments, succeed in family life through their confident leadership. Successful parents base their confidence in knowing they have this sacred mission to carry out with their growing children. They see themselves *raising adults, not children.* They see themselves called by God to carry out a most holy task: to lead their children, through daily self-sacrificing effort, to grow into confident, responsible, considerate, generous men and women who are committed to live by their parents' principles all their lives.

Being conscious of this sacred mission, holding their children's future lives always before their eyes, is what turns these parents into great men and women themselves, real heroes to their children, and makes their family life together a great, rollicking, beautiful adventure.

So, effective parent leaders look at their children and picture them twenty years from now, as grown men and women living life on their own. They seem to understand a truth of life: Children will tend to grow *up* to our expectations or *down* to them. So, these parent leaders set high ideals for their children's later lives. They think of their children's future along these lines:

• The children will have excellent judgment, especially in the choice of a spouse and the upbringing of their own children.

• They will center their lives in a stable, permanent, happy marriage—raising a great family like the one they grew up in.

• They will succeed in their careers, whatever these may be, including (for daughters who choose this) full-time dedication to the family at home—doing work they enjoy, putting their powers up against problems for the welfare of others.

• They'll be able to support their families comfortably but not luxuriously, for a life of excess, they know, may destroy their children (the parents' grandchildren).

• They will be generous to friends and those in need.

• They will have lifelong respect for the opposite sex, and see sex itself as sacred.

• They will never live as quitters, slackers, whiners, or cowards, nor will they let their own children live this way.

• They will be nobody's fool or pushover. They will not be swayed by charlatans. They will know malarkey when they see it.

• When they've done wrong, they'll face the truth and apologize. They will not let their pride stand in the way of truth and justice, especially in family life.

• They will be esteemed by all who know them for their honesty, integrity, hard work, generosity, religious commitment, and confident good humor.

• They will remain close to their brothers and sisters for life, giving and receiving encouragement and support.

• They will live by their parents' principles. They'll have a conscience for life—the voice of their parents' lessons about right and wrong—and they'll pass these lessons on to their own children.

• They will take their religious faith seriously and practice it joyfully. They will strive to love God with all their heart, soul, mind, and strength.

• Their whole lives will be moved by love—the willingness to endure and overcome anything for the welfare and happiness of others, starting with their family and culminating in their love for God.

All leaders understand, and shun, the lamentable consequences of neglect

Consider this: Public monuments are never set up to honor someone who *intended* to do something.

Leaders act. Though they spend time in study and planning, they mostly act. For leaders, study and planning are a ramp-up for action, not a substitute for it.

Moreover, real leaders never let indecision lead to inaction. When confronted with several tough choices of what to do, they do not shrink back. They brace themselves, choose what they judge as the best way forward, and then set to work as best they can.

Sometimes great leadership means just this: doing the best you can with what you have. If you're climbing a mountain, you sometimes have to backtrack or scramble over obstacles or thrash your way through tangled shortcuts; but as long as you keep pushing upward, relying on your compass, you'll reach the summit. The one thing you don't do is quit. Neglect—to do nothing—is the worst mistake of all.

Parent leaders, too, understand the consequences of neglect. They know they have a job to do, a change to effect, in the minds and hearts of their growing children. And they draw courage from foreseeing what awful things could happen to their kids if that job remains undone, if their children retain the flaws and selfishness of childhood into adult life. For instance . . .

• If our children remain self-centered—"Me first!"—they will neglect or mistreat others, and their marriages and careers will fly apart. If their marriages break up, we would lose our grandchildren, or our grandchildren would grow up in a fatherless home.

• If our children have no conscience as a moral compass, they will have no inner force to resist temptation. They could cave in to peer-pressures and meet with disasters: drugs, alcohol abuse, recreational sex, trouble with the law.

• If they never learn to say *please* and *thank you* on their own, without prompting, they will remain self-centered ingrates. They will neglect or mistreat their spouses and think the world owes them a living.

• If they do not respect their parents' authority, they'll have trouble with all other rightful authority: teachers, employers, the law, God Himself.

• If they receive no life-directing guidance from their parents in childhood, they may desperately need guidance later from parent-substitutes: marriage counselors, physicians, mental-health professionals, even cult gurus.

• If they see life as mostly play, they will treat the automobile as a toy. If they cannot control their tempers, they will fly headlong into "road rage" and treat the car as a weapon. Either way, they could kill or cripple themselves and others.

• If they form no principled framework for assessing people's character, they may marry jerks.

• If they cannot manage their own affairs, they cannot take care of others.

• If they do not keep their promises, they cannot keep commitments—not to spouse, or children, or employers.

• If they never learn to set and meet goals, they cannot set and meet ideals.

• If they form a habit of lying, they will someday get fired.

• If they never learn to balance healthy work and play, their lives could shuttle between drudgery and debauchery. If they never learn to be service-oriented producers, they will live as lifelong adolescent consumers.

- If they remain lazy and sloppy in work, they'll get shoved aside by their competition.
- If they see work as "hassle" to be shunned, they will have wobbly, precarious careers. Or they will see work as adolescents see it, as just a source of "spending money."
- If they always expect to have their way, their adult lives will be ravaged by rage and frustration, and their marriages will implode.
- If they sulk and bear grudges, they will muddle through life as smoldering, self-pitying "victims," and they'll never amount to anything.
- If they remain as egocentric children, they may shun having children of their own.
- If they do not stand for something, they will fall for anything.
- If their religious faith remains weak and shallow, they could lose it altogether, along with their immortal souls.
- If they do not find God in their parents' lives, they may never find Him at all.

Leaders are confident of their authority, which is as weighty as their responsibility

Authority means the right (or, if you will, the power) to make decisions and then impose them in order to carry out some responsibility. Leaders have rights because they have duties.

In other words, authority derives directly from responsibility and must be proportional to it, no more and no less. Irresponsible authority is tyranny; inadequate authority leads to anarchy and frustration.

In a real sense, responsible leadership is a form of service. Consequently, rightful authority is both benevolent and beneficial. Leaders in any enterprise serve their people, often at great sacrifice, by constructing order out of chaos and by channeling people's best efforts toward some worthy goal. This is why service-oriented leaders are esteemed by their people, often with deep respect and even devotion.

In light of all this, how do parent leaders see their role of rightful authority in the family?

Smart parents understand that parenthood is not an elective office, and so they do not have to curry favor with their children. Their rights as a parent come with the job, with their huge responsibility. Nobody in any human endeavor, including the family, can bear responsibility without holding the power to carry it out.

It's a fact: parents shoulder an enormous responsibility. They are responsible for their children's welfare, both now and in the future, and for this they answer to the law, to society, to their conscience, and to their Creator. In fact—and this is something parents seldom think about—they will even answer later to their grown children. Someday the children will look back and judge Mom and Dad, up or down, for the way they dealt with them in childhood. (And, by the way, so will their children's spouses.)

So when a man and woman become parents, they take on rights as well. They confidently claim the authority—the power to decide and impose—that they must possess to lead their children responsibly, to keep them from harm, not just now but also later in life.

Authority means, among other things, the right to be obeyed. Smart parents will often harbor quiet doubts and uncertainties about many choices in family life, but they never doubt their right to their children's obedience. They assert this right, as they assert all their other rights, in a clear, no-nonsense way. But this they do with understanding and affection, for all their parental leadership is motivated by love. They're "affectionately assertive" with their children, and this stance is the essence of parental leadership. (See Chapter 6.)

Leaders have joiners, not followers

In World War II, someone asked General Dwight D. Eisenhower the secret of effective leadership. Eisenhower took a piece of string and stretched it out on top of his desk. He said, "Watch. If I try to push the string, it resists and bunches up and goes nowhere. But if I take it by one end and pull it, like this, I can lead it anywhere I want. To lead effectively means to *get out in front and pull. . . .*"

All great leaders get out in front and strive toward some noble goal, and they motivate others to join them. They inspire others to reach that ideal with them, all together in a spirit of adventurous teamwork. In other words, leaders rely on the power of "We. . . ". They make no demands of others that they fail to make of themselves. They lead mostly by example.

Great parents, too, lead their children by example. They sense that children learn character strengths (the virtues) mostly by imitating people they admire, starting with their parents.

So they strive to live as men and women of strong conscience and character. Deliberately, on purpose, they try to live like the kind of adults that they want their children to become—people of judgment, responsibility, courage, self-mastery, faith, hope, and charity. They live this way and expect their children to *join* them.

Consequently, all the rules in the family begin with the word "We. . . ". That is, the parents live by the same standards of upright conduct that they demand of their children. (See Chapter 5.)

Leaders have both the strategic vision and the tenacity to focus on the job at hand

Savvy, effective parents seem to grasp the job they have with their children. That is, they know what they are doing, or at least know where they are going. They have a compass. From time to time they're unsure of tactical details, but they keep their eye on the strategy—the general direction of family life—and this keeps them going despite their occasional (and inevitable) mistakes and shortcomings. Somehow, in the long run, this works.

The strategic thinking of effective parent leaders seems to go like this. . . .

(1) An ancient adage about child-raising says, "As the twig is bent, so grows the tree." This reference to twigs and trees underscores an important fact of life: Raising children right is not an engineering problem. It's not a task with rational steps, clearly connected components, and theoretically under perfect control. Rather, it's more like an agricultural problem. That is, most of the time certain tried-and-true approaches work effectively, but at some point the process of raising kids blurs into mystery—and, like the mysterious growth of crops from seeds, is essentially beyond control. To look at it another way, a parent, like a farmer, does the very best he or she knows how, and then leaves the rest in the hands of God.

(2) Smart fathers and mothers sense that most parents who fail with their kids seem to fall into two extremes. They're either irresponsibly permissive or tyrannically overbearing— either wimps or control freaks. Both extremes are basically self-centered and very often do serious, lasting damage to children. Kids with such parents tend to grow up as either immature narcissists or rebels and sneaks. Loving, self-sacrificing parents, on the other hand, do not fall into extremes: they will not neglect their parental duty to lead, nor will they impose

more control than their children need. Effective parents respect their children's freedom without being permissive, and they work to form their kids but not to dominate them. They put their children's welfare ahead of comfort and ego.

(3) Their number-one job, they see, is to build inner strengths in their children—powers of judgment, conscience, will, and habitual action—that will last a lifetime. This takes years of loving leadership, ongoing teamwork with one's spouse, and patiently persevering effort. They know that kids cannot start acquiring character overnight at age thirteen, the onset of adolescence. What youngsters internalize in childhood will powerfully sway how well or badly they live as teens and young adults.

(4) Parents have to teach their children that responsible grown-up life is not self-centered play (the attitude of children), but mostly *service to others*. The whole of moral development means moving from "self" to "others." They know their kids will grow up not when they can take care of themselves (a common myth), but only when they can *take care of others—and want to.*

(5) Parents can't teach this or anything else important to their children unless the kids *respect* their parents and their rightful authority. It's not enough that they like Mom and Dad; they must also respect them, and nobody respects a play-oriented "buddy" or a shadowy, passive figure around the house—an apparent weakling.

(6) All respect in life, at any age, arises from some perception of strength: physical, moral (judging right from wrong), and intellectual (telling truth from falsehood). So children need to know their parents thoroughly and witness their strong character in action. In family life, the more that children witness and experience their parents' strengths of judgment, will, and action—all motivated by love—the more they will respect Mom and Dad.

(7) As they grow up, children need heroes to emulate, and they eagerly seek these out. They ask themselves, "Who lives a great life? Whom do I want to be like?" For the most part, children grow in character by unconsciously imitating people they admire, starting at home with their parents.

(8) If Mom and Dad are both strong, confident, loving leaders, the children will likely pattern their own lives after them. The more highly kids admire Dad and Mom, the more deeply will they adopt their parents' attitudes, values, and character.

(9) But if their parents are weak non-leaders, living as passive "consumers" without a mission to carry out in family life, then the kids will pattern themselves after other attractive figures instead: the clownish performers and "celebrities" of the entertainment industry. They will be suckers for sales pitches, whether for gadgets or loony ideas or lifestyles. And when pressured by peers, they'll be pushovers.

(10) In other words, smart parent leaders sense that they must work real change in the lives of their children. Kids do not come into the world with strong character. So if a man and his wife neglect this task and effect no change, the kids grow older without growing up. They emerge into adult life with the flaws and weaknesses of childhood. They remain spoiled, vain, domineering, inconstant, impulsive, self-centered, irresponsible—and headed for calamitous careers and marriages.

(11) Smart parents will never permit this to happen. They love their children too much to let them grow up with their faults uncorrected. So they take action now to save their children from future harm.

(12) Time passes ever more quickly. Every decade of life passes twice as fast as the one before, and kids grow older with startling swiftness. Parents know they have only a short time, a tiny window of opportunity, to shape their children's

conscience and character for life. So the parents' mission is not only important, it's also absolutely urgent. Smart parents know they have one chance—and only one—to raise their children right.

ISSUES FOR REFLECTION AND DISCUSSION

(1) This chapter mentions that raising children is a kind of "agricultural" problem, more like farming than engineering. That is, you do the very best you can with certain tried-and-true measures and then rely on "mystery." You put the whole enterprise in God's hands and let Him do His mysterious work.

To extend this analogy: In farming, *timing* is absolutely necessary. No matter what techniques a farmer chooses to use, he absolutely must plow fields and plant his seeds in April, not September, or else he'll meet with famine. He has flexibility with methods but not with the calendar.

How does this question of timing pertain to raising children?

(2) Please comment: In the normal course of human affairs, what circumstances lead some people to be confident? Aside from some people's inborn temperament, it would seem to be these things. . .

a. They grew up in a family surrounded by love.

b. They have a lifelong habit of attacking and solving problems, mostly with success. So they know they have at least a fighting chance in the face of adversity.

c. They have a habit since childhood of turning concerns into corrective action; they are neither deterred by hardship nor paralyzed by worry.

d. They undertake a mission so important that it brings out the best in them.

e. They know that someplace on this earth they have loved ones who are absolutely crazy about them.

f. They sense they are carrying out the will of God.

(3) Below are some descriptive definitions of leaders. How does each tie in with the role of parents as family leaders?

a. "A leader is a dealer in hope" (Napoleon).

b. A leader has, and conveys, wisdom—the ability to assess priorities and know which problems to ignore.

c. A leader makes things happen that would otherwise not happen.

d. A leader is one who can get people to do what they don't want to do (but must do) and like it.

e. A leader establishes a personal identity with his cause.

f. A leader has profound respect and sympathy for those he leads.

g. A leader knows when to listen, when to explain, and when to act.

h. A leader sets standards and rules, but also knows when to make sensible exceptions.

i. A leader is willing occasionally to stand alone.

j. A leader has to have a great heart, a clear mind, and a thick skin.

CHAPTER FIVE

The Power of "We . . ."

The word "We . . ." is a powerful force in family life. It's what anchors children's loyalty to their parents and brothers and sisters, and forges a lifelong bond to their parents' convictions of right and wrong. It empowers children's inner voice of conscience for life.

Family loyalty, it seems, saves many teens and young adults from disaster. Well-raised young people will shun drugs and drunkenness and reckless driving, not only because these are wrong, but because, if caught, the teens would disgrace their family. Fear of causing shame to their family can steel the will of young people, lead them to shrug off peer pressures, say "no" to selfish impulses, and live rightly.

How does this loyalty come about? Through the power of "We. . .".

Every healthy sporting-adventure family lives by a set of clear rules in the home, some high standards for service-centered attitudes and conduct. When kids live by these standards every day for years, they gradually—with fits and starts along the way—internalize powers of judgment, ethical responsibility, gutsy perseverance, and consideration for others. Active family rules cement the kids' rock-hard foundation in place and form the framework for their growth in character.

Why does a healthy family have rules? For one simple reason: because it has a *job* to do, a *service mission* to carry out. A consumerist family, by contrast, has no job at all, for consumption is a static pastime, not an achievement, and so it has no reason to lay down standards for performance.

If we look at the parental job from a professional point of view—that is, the way things work in any serious business enterprise—here's what we see. . . .

Every serious enterprise—whether a business, a non-profit service, a society and its government, or a family—has three basic elements that distinguish it from a loose and pointless or amateurish operation:

• First, a *mission*. This is some long-term goal of service, a task carried out for the betterment of others.

• Second, a *responsible chain of command*. In any group, some people assume the burden of responsibility and consequently hold the authority to lead; they teach and direct others to carry out the institution's mission and deliver its service. In this way, responsible leaders direct those who work with them, not just under them—for, as we've seen before, real leaders have joiners, not followers.

• Third, a *set of performance standards*. These are clear directional rules by which those in charge show others what's expected of them, that is, the ways they most effectively contribute to the overall mission. In business this includes a job description and some sort of protocol that sets standards for satisfactory performance: office rules, by-laws, contractual obligations, and the like.

Here's the point. Every healthy family is a serious service enterprise, and so it displays all three elements outlined here: mission, leadership, and performance standards.

Since the consumerist family is going noplace—has no real directed mission—then the parents are weak leaders (lead where?) and rules, if any, act only as *ad hoc* bandages to keep hassles and damage to a minimum.

As we've seen so far, a father and mother take on a serious mission in family life. Because they assume this huge responsibility, Dad and Mom have the right and duty to lead. All children need leadership, and if both parents do not lead them to do right, then someone else may lead them to do wrong.

In my many conversations with great parents and their children, I used to probe from time to time to learn what rules each healthy family lived by.

Here is what I noticed. . . .

• All the rules, directly or implicitly, began with the word "We . . .," not "You . . ." For instance, the rule for chores was not "*You kids* must clean your room," but, rather, "*We* all pitch in to keep this house in decent shape." Not "*You* must call if you're late," but instead "*We* call if we're going to be late." It wasn't "*You* have to put toys away," but "*We* all return things where they belong."

In other words, *the parents lived by the rules themselves, the same ones they imposed on their children.* The parents lived at home like responsible, considerate adults, and they insisted their kids do the same. Like any other real leaders, Dad and Mom demanded as much of themselves as of their children. They practiced what they preached and led the way by their personal example. Consequently, every day, their children witnessed the parents' convictions alive in ongoing action. (And so, later as teenagers, they could never justly accuse their parents of hypocrisy.)

• Abiding by these rules led the children—or forced them—to practice each of the virtues. Repeatedly, every day, Dad and Mom encouraged their children to live rightly: to take responsibility, manage their own affairs, work conscientiously, discern right from wrong, respect their parents' authority, and consider the needs and rights and feelings of others. Right living permeated the whole spirit of the family and seeped its way inside the kids little by little, day by day. An old maxim says, "As the day goes, so goes one's life." Whatever the children practice every day, for good or for ill, will be the way they live later.

• In a sense, the dynamic by which children learned the virtues through these rules seemed to follow the wise adage: What children *hear*, they mostly forget. What they *see*, they mostly remember. What they *do*, they understand and internalize.

• All the rules seemed to fall into five distinct but interconnected categories:

—We respect the rights and sensibilities of others.

—We all contribute to making our home a clean, orderly, civilized place to live.

—We give people information they need to carry out their responsibilities.

—We use electronic media only to promote family welfare, never to work against it.

—We love and honor our Creator above all things; we thank Him for His blessings and ask His help for our needs and those of others.

For whatever use they may be to you, I list these rules for you here. Once again let me stress, what I lay out below is *de*scriptive, not *pre*scriptive. That is, I am describing what I've seen work in one great family after another. I do not presume to dogmatize about details here, or insist that every family should adopt these standards wholesale. I couldn't rightly do that even if I wanted to.

Let me stress, too, that practically no family lives by each and every one of these rules. I have simply listed all of them here for your thoughtful judgment.

It's up to you to weigh each one and judge what's best for you and your children. It's your family, and therefore your call.

Here they are. . . .

1. *We respect the rights and sensibilities of others.*

• We say to everyone, when appropriate: *please, thank you, excuse me, I'm sorry, I give my word of honor.*
• We do not insult people with words or affront them with rudeness.
• We do not tattletale or gossip about people, or otherwise negatively criticize people behind their backs. (Though if someone we know is getting involved with drugs, then for their sake we report it to whoever can help them in time.)
• We keep our family's affairs within the family. No "airing dirty laundry in public."
• We make no disparaging remarks of a racist, sexist, ethnic, or religious nature, not even as a joke. We have no place in our home for humor that hurts.
• We do not use profanity or vulgar language.
• We never ridicule or belittle anyone who tries.
• We do not interrupt; we wait our turn to speak. We do not distract people when they're speaking with someone, either in person or on the phone. If there's an urgent situation and we must interrupt, then we first say, "Excuse me, please. . . ."
• We respect people's right to presumption of innocence. Before forming a negative judgment, we first listen to their side of things.
• We never lie to each other. Unless we have rock-solid evidence to the contrary, we presume other family members tell the truth.
• We do not argue back when we are corrected.

• We do not make promises unless we commit ourselves to carry them out. If we can't keep a promise for reasons beyond our control, then we make a sincere apology.

• We respect each other's property and right to privacy. We knock before entering a closed room; we ask permission before borrowing something.

• We do not bicker or quarrel during meals.

• If we must get up from the table at meals, we first say, "Excuse me, please."

• We greet adult friends of our family with good manners, a warm greeting, a friendly handshake and look in the eye. We give our guests the best of what we have. (But children do not talk with adult strangers without parents' OK.)

• We show special respect to older people. We offer to give them a seat, hold doors for them, let them go first in line.

• We celebrate each other's accomplishments. But win or lose, we appreciate each other's best efforts.

• We practice good telephone manners and thus bring honor to our family. We keep use of the telephone under reasonable control:

—No telephone calls during dinner or homework or after 10:00 P.M.

—No outgoing telephone calls after 9:30 P.M. (except for emergencies).

—Telephone calls are generally limited to fifteen minutes.

2. *We all contribute to making our home a clean, orderly, civilized place to live.*

• We do not enter the house with wet or muddy footwear; if we track in a mess, we clean it up right away.

• We do not bring "outdoor" activities indoors: no running and chasing, ball-playing, missile throwing, rough wrestling, or excessive shouting. Males in the family wear no hats or caps indoors.

• We open and close doors quietly; if we accidentally slam a door, we say, "Excuse me, please."

• We do not shout messages to people in other rooms. We walk to wherever someone is and then deliver the message in a normal voice.

• We do not consume food outside of designated eating areas: kitchen, dining room, play or TV room.

• We do not overindulge in food or drink. No unauthorized snacks between meals, especially right before meals.

• We try to eat all the food set before us.

• At night, we lay out clothes for use the next morning.

• We put clothes where they belong when not in use: clean clothes in closet or drawers, dirty clothes in laundry.

• When we're finished with them, we put toys, sports gear, and tools back where they belong.

• If we've used a plate or drinking glass, we rinse or clean it and put it where it belongs.

• If we've borrowed something, we return it. If we've lost a borrowed item, we apologize and try our best either to replace it or pay for it.

• We do our house chores promptly and to the best of our ability; we start our homework at a set time and stick with it until it's done right.

• We do not return a car home with less than a quarter-tank of gas.

• We can all make suggestions about many affairs in family life, but parents make decisions in serious matters. And they decide what's serious.

• We do not aim for "results" as such, but rather for *personal best effort.*

3. *We give people information they need to carry out
their responsibilities.*

• When we're going out, we always inform: where we are
going, with whom, and when we plan to return.
• We get prior permission, with at least one day's notice,
for important and potentially disruptive activities: sleepovers,
camping trips, long distance trips, and the like.
• We come straight home from school, work, social events
—except with prior consultation.
• We return from social events at a reasonable hour, one
previously agreed upon.
• If we're going to be late, we call.
• We take phone messages intelligently: name of caller,
caller's name and phone number, summary of message (if
any), time and date of call, name or initials of person who
took the call.
• In general, we work to avoid unpleasant surprises and
unnecessary worry in the family. (We have enough as it is.)

4. *We use electronic media and games only to promote
family welfare, never to work against it.*

• We have one television in the house, so as to monitor it
and keep it from fragmenting the family.
• We use TV and video-gadgets sparingly and discerningly. Most of our recreation will be non-electronic: reading,
games, hobbies, sports, or conversation.
• We permit nothing in our home that offends our moral
principles and treats other human beings as things: no pornography (treating women as objects), no racist or sexist or
ethnic disparagement, no gratuitous violence, no coarse language, no glamorous depictions of disrespect and rudeness.
• We will usually—not always, but much of the time—

watch TV and movies together: sports, high quality shows and films, news and documentaries. That's it.

• We do not watch TV on school nights, unless we watch together or with prior consultation, as noted above.

• If we bicker over TV or games, we get one warning to stop; if quarreling persists, the activity is terminated.

• We keep noise level within reason so as not to distract or bother others.

5. *We love and honor our Creator above all things; we thank Him for His blessings and ask His help for our needs and those of others.*

• We thank the Lord by worshipping Him together as a family.

• We strive to live by His commandments of right and wrong.

• We respect the conscience and rights of others who worship Him differently.

• We pray before meals and bedtime. We pray for the needs of our family and country and those of anyone suffering in sorrow. We serve the Lord by serving others.

• We live in the confidence that God watches over us with His loving fatherly protection. Parents treat their children the way God treats all of us—with affectionate and protective love, attention to needs, clear standards of right and wrong, compassionate understanding, and a ready willingness to forgive.

• We know that God commands all of us to honor father and mother. The finest way we do this is to adopt our parents' values, live by them all our lives, and pass them on to our own children whole and intact.

* * *

There you have them, the rules most commonly found in great families.

To live by them perfectly every day is, of course, an impossible ideal. Some backsliding and flawed performance is absolutely normal, for both parents and children. Nobody's perfect. All the same, these rules are fixed in place as what we try to live by, a "resting place" for our conscience—like the keys on a piano or computer keyboard to which our fingers always return. A great family never attains perfection, but it will never stop trying. To keep trying, no matter what, is the essence of greatness.

ISSUES FOR REFLECTION AND DISCUSSION

(1) Please go through the list of rules (standards) outlined above and choose whichever would best suit your family's circumstances. Are there any you would add?

(2) In what ways do these rules impart, by example and directed practice, the great character-strengths? How do they help children to "see the invisible"?

(3) They say, "Reaching an ideal is nearly impossible, but to *try* is *always* possible." Given that living perfectly by these rules is nearly impossible, why is it important that parents emphasize "personal best effort" in family life, for themselves as well as their children? And how does this relate to apology and forgiveness?

(4) Please comment on this: If you prepare children to have a great marriage and family life (which is what these rules do), you're also preparing them to have a great career— for the character that leads someone to form a stable, happy marriage also makes him or her a successful professional. How would many of these rules, with appropriate changes, apply just as well in business and professional life?

(5) Do you agree with this statement? Children are disinclined to "take orders" from parents unless they see the *whole family* "take orders" from some higher ethic, ultimately from God.

(6) The divorce rate for couples today hovers around 50 percent. But among those who practice their religion seriously, it's less than 2 percent. What accounts for this?

CHAPTER SIX

Discipline: Affectionate Assertiveness

In recent times, the word "discipline" has had a bad press. It's widely misunderstood to mean punishment. But discipline does not mean punishment. Nor does it mean enforcing rules just for the sake of minimizing hassles at home, a kind of "damage control."

Discipline certainly involves occasional punishment and assertive control as well as clear guidelines for behavior. But its real meaning is deeper and more important. Discipline really means confident, effective parental leadership.

Look at it this way. The word "discipline" is related to the word "disciple," and it springs from the Latin word meaning "to learn." Discipline is what happens when some leader teaches and his "disciples" learn. Broadly speaking, discipline means teaching and learning, leading and joining along.

To repeat the key idea here, discipline in family life means leading the children to acquire—by personal example, directed practice, and verbal explanation (in that order)—the great virtues of sound judgment, a sense of responsibility, personal courage, self-control, and magnanimity. These powers take root in the give-and-take of family life and then flower to healthy maturity through the steady nourishment of confident, unified parental leadership. All this takes years.

So, discipline (teaching) requires planning and patience as much as occasional swift corrective action. It calls for giving example as much as giving rules, and encouragement and praise as much as loving denial and just punishment.

For parents, it means living in the family in such a way that children are led to do what is right—as the parents see this—

93

and shun what is wrong, and to explain the differences so compellingly that the children will remember the lessons all their lives and then pass them on to their own children. That's the long and the short of it.

Affectionate assertiveness

Consistently, effective parents practice what we might call *affectionate assertiveness*. That is, the parents *assert* correct conduct and attitudes by their example, action, and words. At the same time, they're unfailingly affectionate with their children. They correct their children because they love them, want to protect them, and care above all else for their future welfare and happiness.

They set out to *correct the fault, not the person.* They "hate the sin, love the sinner." They're willing, on occasion, to risk being temporarily "unpopular" with a wayward son or daughter—knowing that their future happiness is at stake and that their children will someday thank them and revere them as great parents.

How do you show affectionate love to your children?

You physically touch them. You welcome them on your knee and embrace them. You take them by the hand while walking together. You playfully squeeze them on the arm or shoulder. When walking by them, you pat them on the head or ruffle their hair a bit. You invite them to sit next to you and pat them when they sit down. You greet them a wink and a smile. You tell corny jokes and laugh at theirs. You tell funny stories and find other ways to share a good laugh, but without offending anyone. You whisper things in their ears. (Sometimes, when you feel like shouting something at your small children, have them sit on your lap instead and whisper it into their ear. This seldom fails to get their attention, and your correction comes across affectionately, as it should.)

You show happiness and pride in their accomplishments. *You make praise every bit as specific as blame.* Parents tend to make blame specific but to put praise in vague generalities: "You've been a good girl this morning. . . ." Praise them for a job well done, even when they've done it as punishment: "You did a great job making your bed this morning. . . . Your room is spic-and-span, just the way it should be. . . . Your homework looks neat and professional, and I'm proud of you. . . ." Children need sincere praise from time to time. In fact, we all do. One of people's greatest needs, at any age, is sincere appreciation.

When you tuck them into bed, you linger a bit, just a couple of minutes to make small talk. Bedtime is a great occasion to talk things over with children, and listen to them. All their lives, they will fondly remember their bedtime chats with Mom and Dad.

Most of all, with both sons and daughters, you show affection with your eyes. You should *listen to your children with your eyes.* When you deliberately make eye-contact with them, especially when they're speaking to you, you show how much you care for them. In your eyes they can read your soul— your love for them, your pride in them, your hopes for their future.

Somehow, mysteriously, normal children sense when their parents correct them out of love. Great parents correct *because* they love. Even though kids dislike and resist the correction itself, deep down they grasp the love behind their parents' direction. Sooner or later, as they grow up, they understand that their parents' occasional wrath is aimed at their conduct, not them personally.

Since you, as a parent, show plenty of affection in normal situations of family life (which is most of the time), and because you always show willingness to forgive once apologies are made and punishment done, your children sense the truth—that your whole life, including episodes of corrective punishment, is devoted to their happiness. Later, as young adults, and even before they're out of their teens, they will fully understand why your love moved you to act as you did, and they will thank you.

So, these things being said, what can you do to punish misbehavior in fairly serious matters? Here is a list drawn from parents' experience:

• With very young children, physically restrain them. Take them by the hand or arm and remove them to someplace private. Take both hands or wrists in yours, hold them still, and look them straight in the eye. Say what you have to say in a low but "I-mean-business" way and keep at it until they've understood and said they are sorry.

• Remove them physically and make them spend what some parents call "time out"—a few minutes of isolation away from the family, even in a closed room. Don't let them return until they've said they're sorry. (For very young children, you may have to supervise their time in a corner or some other "punishment spot.")

• For older children and preteens, remove privileges. This means no games or television or use of the phone. For teens it might mean no phone calls or going out with friends or use of the car. (Teens who display thoughtless, uncontrolled impulse are a menace on the road and shouldn't drive anyway. You should make this clear to them: only considerate, responsible adults may drive the family car.)

• Put them to work. Have a so-called "job jar" at home. This is a receptacle with slips of paper describing jobs to be done around the house. Let the malefactor pick out three slips and then choose one job, which must then be done to your satisfaction. Also, if kids complain they're "bored" around the house, direct them to the job jar. Parents who do this seldom hear complaints from their kids about boredom. The word "boring" disappears from the family vocabulary.

• If two siblings are quarreling and won't stop after one warning, put both of them to work on the same project: cleaning dishes, raking leaves, gardening, washing the car, whatever. This treatment usually effects a reconciliation. Misery loves company.

A parenthesis here: For many kids in consumerist families, being banished to the bedroom is scarcely a punishment at all. Typically, kids' rooms bulge with stereos, radio, television, and electronic games galore, and the kids live like sultans. Their rooms are essentially entertainment centers surrounding a bed.

In contrast, many healthy families hold to this policy: each child's bedroom is a place for study, reading, chatting and playing with siblings, and sleep. Entertainment gadgets are only for common areas of the house, where people can enjoy them together. This policy has the happy side effect of banishing electronic distractions from homework. It works. And the kids learn a truth about life: When we try to work and play at the same time, we wind up doing neither. Leisure is really enjoyable only when we've earned it.

In any event, whatever method of correction you use with your small children, see it as an investment that will later yield high return. Once you've established your authority in their youngest years, then you've won most of the struggle. When they're older, just a businesslike warning or flashing-eyed glare from you, or even telling them you're "disappointed," usually works to restore cooperation. By that time, the kids know you mean business. In child-rearing as in law (and especially with the IRS), there are few things as effective as a sincere threat.

"Memorable correction"

Smart parents—those who practice this affectionate assertive-ness—work with each other to plan out different "memorable lessons" of responsibility (that is, punishments) in response to their children's varying types of misbehavior. This is impor-tant. The more carefully these responses are thought out be-forehand, and thus made routine in family life, the calmer and more consistent both parents are in handling their kids' provocations.

This rational structure avoids, or at least minimizes, the problem in many ineffective families, especially when dealing with teenagers—impromptu punishments imposed in anger, often harsh and overreactive, and resented (with some justice) as unfair.

Remember, you can be tough with normal children and quite effective with them if, and only if, they perceive that you're trying to be fair.

Here is a rational structure for imposing memorable cor-rection on the kids for their wayward ways. It's based on a sound principle from military history: Those generals who chose their battlegrounds ahead of time usually emerged as winners—Hannibal at Cannae, Wellington at Waterloo, Lee at Fredericksburg, Eisenhower at Normandy.

Choose your battleground. Don't scatter your resources trying to correct the children every single time they do wrong. If you tried this, you'd soon need to be fitted for a straitjacket.

Instead, establish three levels of misbehavior, each calling for suitably heavy response. In rising order of seriousness, these are:

First, *misdemeanors*. These are minor infractions, just kiddish misdeeds arising from children's inexperience, thoughtless-ness, and reckless impulse—such as tracking mud in the house, noisy rough-housing, throwing missiles indoors, forgetting (that is, honestly forgetting) to do chores, failing to put things away. A lot of these habits the kids will outgrow anyway. Minor misdeeds like these call for quick but low-level response, and sometimes just letting the matter go. It's like the quality-control system in a factory: try to catch a sample every few times. You don't need to correct misdemeanor goofs every single time, and you might go crazy if you tried.

Second, *serious infractions.* These are acts where children infringe on the rights of others, especially siblings: causing offense by name-calling, taking property without permission, physical aggression, refusing to give or accept apology, using profanity, and similar deeds of injustice. Though you can occasionally, even fairly often, overlook the misdemeanors mentioned above, you *must* correct these serious lapses of justice and charity practically every single time.

Never forget, every single time you correct your children's infringements on the rights of others, you are forming their lifelong conscience and ethics. You are preparing them for the way they will later treat their spouses, children, and professional colleagues. So there is a lot at stake here. Don't give up.

Third, *felony infractions.* These are serious matters that endanger your children's welfare, either now or later in life, and they call for the severest punishment every single time, whatever this might be. The kids should have the roof fall in on them.

For the youngest children this category obviously includes whatever physically endangers them: playing with fire, wandering into the street, poking metal objects into electrical outlets, and the like. Punishment should be swift and memorable. It seems that nearly all parents, even the most pacifist, react this way through sheer protective instinct.

But equally important are those wrongdoings that threaten children's welfare later on in life—those acts and attitudes that imperil their basic concepts of respect for rightful authority and the importance of personal integrity. You must impose swift, serious punishment every time your children do the following:

• Show disrespect for you personally—call you names, try to strike you, raise their voice in anger at you, say that they "hate" you.

• Attempt to defy your authority—say "no" or otherwise refuse to comply with your clear direction, or deliberately "forget" to do so. This pertains even in relatively minor matters, especially after you've given warning. For instance, if you direct your son to clean up a mess of his and he refuses or just walks away, then the issue becomes one of authority, not just clean-up. You must not permit him to get away with this defiance.

• Deliberately lie to you (and you know this for a fact), especially after being put on their honor to tell the truth.

These three areas are vitally important for your children's welfare. *Everything you have to teach your children depends on their respect for you and for your authority and for their own word of honor. If you lose this, you lose them.*

Respect for rights

Effective parents combine rightful authority with respect for their children's rights.

Children do have rights, of course. Not because they're children, but because they are people; and all people, even young ones, have certain basic rights. Here are the rights that effective parents keep in mind as they exercise moral leadership in the family:

• *Right to privacy (up to a point).* Older children need a certain security of privacy. For instance, they should have a place of their own to keep personal effects (such as letters and diaries) away from prying by other family members. And their normal, above-board dealings with friends should be respected as "personal," essentially no one's business but theirs.

Naturally, these privacy rights are not absolute, just as they're not absolute in adult society either. Sometimes privacy rights have to give way before higher necessity. For instance, the law can force testimony under oath and it makes allowances for "reasonable search" in criminal investigations.

So, too, in your family. Your children's privacy rights give way to your parental rights wherever some serious danger suggests itself—for example, in possible involvement with drugs, or what you perceive as excessive intimacy with the opposite sex. But in normal circumstances, *parents who respect their children's privacy generally find that their children grow to be open and sincere with them.* If you respect their rights, they will respect your judgment, and then come to you with the truth. Nearly always, it is control-oriented, excessively prying parents who produce children who are close-mouthed, secretive, and sneaky.

• *Right to presumption of innocence.* Don't rush to judgment. Listen to your children's side of things, especially when you're dealing with older children, and most especially when you did not personally witness the alleged misdeed. But by the same token, never, ever, undercut your spouse if it was he or she who witnessed things. If you think your spouse is mistaken or overreactive, then discuss matters privately.

• *Right not to be publicly embarrassed.* Whenever you can, make corrections personally and privately, as you would among your fellow adults. If you chew out your child in front of siblings or friends, the lesson is probably lost. Your child's resentment at public humiliation acts like static to cancel out your message. Corrections made privately, eyeball to eyeball, go straight to the point.

• *Right to just punishment.* An angry, overreactive punishment easily skyrockets way out of proportion to the original provocation. To be effective and long-lasting, to get the lesson across for life, punishment has to be fair. It will be fair if it's rational, and it's rational if thought out carefully beforehand, as mentioned above. Sometimes, in fact, you can even ask your son or daughter to propose a suggestion of their own for reasonable punishment: "What do you think is fair? Make me an offer." More often than not, surprisingly, their proposals turn out to be reasonable, and sometimes even more severe than what you had in mind.

• *Right to a second chance.* This means, once apologies and restitution are forthcoming, the kids start with a clean slate. Children, like all the rest of us, resent grudge-bearing and long memories for past misdeeds that were supposedly forgiven and over with. We do not really forgive unless we also forget. When you truly forgive and forget, you show the kids that it's their misconduct you disapprove of, not them as people. Forgiveness like this is crucial, absolutely indispensable for family solidarity. The family is one place in the world where we can always count on a fresh start.

From time to time, through wrath or oversight, you may blunder in doing justice to your children. Whenever this happens, follow up with an apology.

If you imposed an excessive punishment, then retract it and scale back to whatever seems reasonable. Don't ever be afraid to say "I'm sorry" to your children, and to explain why. Never fear that you'll seem inconsistent in their eyes. You really are being consistent in what matters most, your heartfelt determination to treat them fairly. When you apologize, you teach them a valuable lesson: that you put justice ahead of your ego.

What are we talking about here? In all of this we're really talking about the way responsible grown-ups try to treat each other. You, like anyone else, would expect other adults to respect your rights to privacy, presumption of innocence, personal dignity, just penalty, and so on. You'd expect this treatment from your spouse, your employers, the law. So, *what you're really teaching your children is ethical conduct among responsible adults*. You are treating your children as young adults-in-the-making, and you begin by respecting them as people.

Guidelines from veteran parents

Negative guidelines are as helpful as positive ones, often more so. It's useful for a parent to know what not to do—that is, what to avoid—in a complicated situation.

I used to ask veteran parents (mothers and fathers whose children had grown and gone) what warnings or other "negative know-how" they'd pass on to younger parents in this area of unified moral leadership. In paraphrase, here are some bits of hard-earned wisdom they mentioned:

• To HUSBANDS: Don't neglect your wife. She needs what we all need: understanding, affection, gratitude, support, and appreciation. For sure, she doesn't get these from the children when they're small. So if she doesn't get them from her husband either, then she doesn't get them at all. You can tell you're neglecting your wife if she starts complaining about small things around the house, one after another, circling around and around the central problem: your apparent unconcern for her. Wake up. Pay attention. Listen to her carefully, help her out, tell her she's great, hug and kiss her from time to time—all this goes a long way. Every time you kiss your wife in front of the children, you are, in effect, kissing each of them in turn.

- To WIVES: Don't undercut your husband. Do all you can to lead your children to respect their father and his authority. He simply cannot lead as a father without his children's abiding respect. Your children's growth in character, their lifelong happiness, can rise or fall on how deeply they respect their dad. So lead them, by your example and your praise for him, to view their dad as you do: a great man, a model of masculine strength and accomplishment, a self-sacrificing hero worthy of the whole family's gratitude and honor. Your children's respect for their dad will grow directly from your own esteem for him, and this is crucially important to his influence on their lives.

Listen to this story from a man in the Midwest: "I was the youngest of five children in a single-parent home. My dad died when I was an infant, so I never knew him. My mother raised us as a widow, and she was a great woman. Every now and then, when I was getting out of hand as a boy, and even as a teenager, my Mom would take me aside and say, 'Jimmy, your father would *never approve* of what you're doing right now! He would be very upset. So stop it. . . .' This never failed to touch me, not once. It always brought me to my senses and made me straighten out."

Do you see? The father of this home continued to influence his children for good, even after his death, because of his great wife's love and honor for him. Because he was still alive in her heart, he was still the father of this family.

- Don't underestimate your children. Have high ambitions for their swift, step-by-step growth into maturity. We all tend to become what we think about, and kids tend to become what their parents expect of them. Even when they sometimes let you down and you have to correct them, make them understand that you see this as just a blip along the way. You have no doubt, none whatever, that they'll someday grow into excellent men and women. You're proud of them, confident in them. Always will be.

• Don't treat teenagers like large children. Think of them, and treat them, as near-adults—adults in everything but experience. Pull them up from childhood, fine-tune their consciences, welcome them to adult reality. Show them how to balance a checkbook, pursue a job, work professionally, please their bosses, deal respectfully with the opposite sex. Show them how to buy good clothes, take care of their wardrobe, and dress well. When they complain, "Why don't you trust me?" tell them that you distinguish between *integrity* and *judgment*. You trust their integrity and sense of family honor, their honesty and good intentions—always have, always will. But what you must mistrust for now, in good conscience, is their inexperienced judgment. That is, you will not let them hurt themselves or others through their naïve blunders. When they start showing that they think and act like responsible adults, then you'll trust them right across the board, in judgment as well as integrity.

• Don't ever tell your teens that the high-school years are the best part of their lives. This isn't true. Adolescence, in fact, is one of life's toughest times: coping with blunders and glandular upheavals, crawling up and down learning curves. Tell your teenagers, and above all show them, that every stage of life is interesting, challenging, enjoyable for anyone with a sporting, adventurous spirit. Teens who've been well brought up have a great life ahead of them, like the life they see in you. (Think about it. How many older teens and young adults are tempted to suicide because they believe what they've been told: the best part of life is behind them.)

• Don't let your kids weasel out of commitments. Don't let them take back their word on a whim. Before they make promises or otherwise commit themselves to a course of action, press them to think through the consequences and understand their terms, because you will hold them to their word. If they want to buy a pet, make them first commit themselves to feed and care for it; then hold them to that. If they accept an invitation to a party, they're obligated to attend even if something more alluring turns up. If they want to take guitar lessons, make them promise to persevere, no matter what, for two or more years. When they promise anything, ask them, "Do I have your word on that?"

• Don't ask children if they'd "like" to do something that you expect them to do anyway. Simply tell them firmly and positively of the plan. And similarly, don't ask "OK?" at the end of a directive request—"It's your turn to put the dishes away, OK?" What you mean by this term is "Do you understand?" But they may take it to mean "Do you approve? Is this all right with you?" This misunderstanding can lead to problems.

• When you're correcting your kids and they ask "Why?"—don't argue with them. If they're looking for an explanation, give it once only. If they persist with "Why?" then they're looking for an argument, not an explanation. Close off the matter. In other words, they must take your "no" as an answer, but you don't take theirs. You can dialogue with your children about many issues, but there's no "dialogue" about your rights as a parent.

• Don't be afraid to treat each of your children in different ways, even if this may sometimes seem unfair to siblings. You have to be a realist, and the fact is that youngsters have different temperaments as well as different needs and problems at different ages, all requiring suitably adjusted, custom-tailored treatment. For instance, an aggressive hothead and a sensitive introvert need different styles of handling; what would subdue the one would crush the other. You needn't apologize for this. Just explain it this way: "I'm trying to be fair to everyone, but above all I must address and cope with people's individual needs. A good doctor renders excellent service to all her patients, but not in the same way. Equality of rights doesn't mean sameness of treatment. If this seems unfair to you—and I can understand why it might—just trust me. Someday later, when you have children of your own, you'll understand."

• Don't let your kids dress in such a way as to bring shame to the family. Nobody has a right to do this.

• Don't miss small opportunities to talk with your children. Listen politely and respectfully. You can talk with them while driving, doing dishes and other chores together, walking and biking, working on hobbies you share, tucking them into bed. If you cut down on tube-watching, you'll find slivers and chunks of time here and there. Make the time, and never forget you haven't much of it left; your children will grow up with astonishing swiftness.

• Don't shout at your kids all the time. It's a waste of breath. If one of your kids needs a talking to, take him or her out for a walk or a soda, and say what you have to say in a calm, serious way. Don't forget to listen, either; for your kids' view of things, though wrong, may still have a point. A couple of heart-to-heart talks are better than a dozen explosions.

• Don't get trapped into prolonged blazing arguments, especially with your teens, and most especially if you have a temper. Words can wound and take a long time to heal. If tempers are flaring, put off the discussion till later, that evening or the next day, when you've both cooled down—but avoid the temptation to just drop the matter, or to pile on too many still-unresolved issues. In any event, if you go too far, be the first to apologize. (But by the same token, remember that justly provoked wrath has its uses. On those rare occasions when the kids do something truly outrageous, they should experience outrage. Otherwise they won't know what's outrageous.)

• Don't forget to praise your children, and be specific about it. Kids need a pat on the back from time to time. We all do. Give praise mostly for behavior that you want to reinforce and see repeated: for instance, the way they live the rules of the family. Be very sparing, though, with praise that could just stoke their vanity—praise for those good features they were born with and shouldn't take credit for: good looks, pretty face, lustrous hair, athletic abilities, and the like. Above all, give praise for effort. Teach the kids this adult-life lesson: because success depends on effort, then effort is more important than success. You always appreciate when your children try.

• Come down to your children's level, but don't stay there. Kids are kids, and you have to come down to their level to lead them by the hand. But your long-term goal is to bring them up to your own level—to lead them, patiently over time, to think and act like mature grown-ups. So live like a grown-up. Enjoy being an adult on top of life, and let them see what this means. If they see you enjoy living as a confident, productive adult, they'll have a life to look forward to.

• Don't worry so much about trivia. Many parents worry

too much about making mistakes in trifling details and not enough about the big, long-range issues of character and conscience. If you keep your eyes on your children's futures and steadily try to do the right thing, then your mistakes along the way don't really matter much. Take your cue from the parents of large families. They don't have nearly enough time to worry, hesitate, or split hairs in decisions. They just charge ahead, trust their commonsense parental instincts, and do the best they can—and they succeed. Your children will not remember your mistakes (the things you worry about now); what they will remember fondly, devotedly, is your loving, confident leadership.

• If you're a parent of a large family, don't worry if you seem to lack enough time to spend with each of your children. You need less time than you think, and you give more time than you realize. You're teaching an enormous amount just by your generous example. A big family, it seems, is inherently formative. Children learn a lot from their siblings, receive constant stimulation through conversation, play, and teamwork. Since they're genuinely needed at home, they know their strengths, are more willing to take risks, and thus grow in self-confidence. When doing homework, they're surrounded by distractions—and so they learn to focus their concentration and work almost anywhere. Through give-and-take life with siblings, they learn to get along with all sorts of people. Older children learn responsibility; younger children are surrounded by love. All the children look back as adults on how much sheer fun they had growing up a rollicking, affectionately happy family. And they'll remember how Mom and Dad were great people.

ISSUES FOR REFLECTION AND DISCUSSION

(1) Some observers have noted this phenomenon: In children's most troubled times of life (ages two to five, then again later at thirteen to seventeen), kids will assert themselves to see who's "boss" in the family. They try to wrest control from their parents. If they win in this struggle, they grow out of control themselves. Most of their wildness and anger—fear, really—derives from living in a environment (in this case, a family) where nobody's in control. But when the parents win, when they appear to the children as obviously in loving control, then children grow to feel safe and secure. Confidence in their parents' control forms the basis for their own growth in self-confidence. Comment?

(2) Related to the above, some parents have noted that the problems of adolescence are really a replay of the tangle in the early years, ages two to five: same mood swings, same uncertainties, same push to see how much they can get away with.

In those families where parents win out as "boss" by the time kids are five—that is, when the kids know who's really leading the family—the years of adolescence are relatively untroubled. Parent-leaders find (often to their surprise) that most of the time they enjoy a great relationship with their teenage children.

But when the kids win out as "boss" in the youngest years, their flaws remain intact and then grow monstrous in adolescence. An out-of-control five-year-old is an annoyance; that same child as an out-of-control teenager is a nightmare.

Moral: The relationship between parents and kids in kindergarten, whether healthy or unhealthy, is a preview of what will probably happen in high school. Comment?

(3) We've spoken about the "invisible realities" that children need to learn. One of these is the "invisible line" surrounding each person's rights and dignity. That is, children must grasp that, beyond a certain line, they begin to infringe on others' rights and affront their dignity—and this is what parents won't allow. When children cross that line, they must receive "memorable correction" in the form of punishment. (In a sense, it's like the hidden "electric fence" some people use to keep pets from straying off the property. When pets step across the line, they receive a memorable jolt.) If parents do not point out that line, repeatedly and seriously, then the kids don't know where it is, or even that it exists. They retain the "Me first!" attitude of childhood and think anything can be done for a laugh. Comment?

(4) It's evident that many parents today are afraid to punish their children. What do you think they are really afraid of?

(5) One of the maxims of children's upbringing says, "Correct the fault, not the person." How does this distinction serve to bolster parents' courage when they must punish their children?

(6) See whether you agree with this: The *why* of correction is more important than the *how*. That is, when parents punish their children for the right reason (out of love for the children, for sake of their long-term welfare), then the actual method of punishment isn't so important. Deep down, children sense whether their parents' corrections spring from ego or from love, and this underlying attitude is what they respond to, not the method or even the severity of the punishment. This explains why successful parents can be fairly strict without being tyrannical, or easy-going without being permissive.

(7) Please comment on these pointers from parents about children's upbringing:

  a. Self-denial is a quality built from the outside in. Teach your children this: In adult life, all of us occasionally need to be told NO by somebody: spouse, employers, friends, the police, the IRS. We adults don't like to be corrected either, but we just accept it, learn from it, and move on.

  b. It's important for parents to remind themselves that small children's occasional unruliness is normal and even exceptional. Most of the time they behave reasonably well. We tend to magnify the unruly incidents because they're so annoying.

  c. Often, when adolescents are raising objections to parents' drawing the line between right and wrong, they're really looking for reasoned explanations: *Why* is the line drawn *there* and not someplace else? Because the teens are upset (understandably, for no one likes being corrected), it's easy for parents to underestimate how much effect they're having. Be patient. Despite appearances, they really are listening, and your lessons really are sinking in. In a year or two, to your great surprise, you may overhear your teen giving the same lesson, even in the same words, to a wayward younger sibling. This happens a lot in healthy families.

  d. In our times, the phone has replaced the front door as the main entranceway to the home. So insist that your children use good telephone manners as a way of bringing honor to the family. For that matter, help kids to see that your family is honored every time they show good manners in public, and for this you're proud of them.

e. Keep coming back to fairness. Tell your children this: I'm always open to let you tell me if you think I'm being unfair, on two conditions—first, you give me *reasons why*, and secondly, you tell me *respectfully*.

f. Compliment children for cooperative behavior even when it was forced upon them. Similarly, praise them for a job well done even when it was done as punishment. This lessens the pain and teaches a positive lesson.

g. Your "no" can bolster your teens against peer pressure. Tell them: "Blame us. Tell your friends we'll ground you if you do that. . . ."

h. Consistently, one of the most favorite activities for children is visiting where Dad works. The kids see other adults (co-workers) show friendly esteem for him. They form a more tactile sense of his "power," the place where he does important things. They form greater respect for him as a powerful man. They grow more proud of him.

CHAPTER SEVEN

The Media as Rivals

Teachers hear a plaintive cry over and over again from busy parents, especially dads: "Where can I get time to live with my children? I'm working longer hours than ever, and my kids are always on the go. How can I make more time?"

No easy answers. But here is a help that many parents have found for themselves: When you cut back the intrusion of electronic media in your house, it's remarkable how much more time you create. Imposing some sort of sensible control over TV and other gadgets adds hours each week to family life. It seems that when parents make up their mind and then act to shove the media's distractions out of the house—the noise, the blather, the hours and hours of useless staring— they win more time in the family and bolster their children's respect for them as leaders.

It's like this. Smart parents sense that television and the other electronic doodads—VCR's, computer games, radio, recorded music, the Internet—intrude in the home as *rivals* for their children's attention and respect. When used to excess, the media muscle in as competing authority figures that distract children's minds and hearts. Kids don't pay much attention to parents, and hardly hear or overhear what goes on at home when their gaze fixes for hours each day on a glimmering cathode-ray tube.

But note we use the term *rivals* here, not *enemies*. When wisely used, the media can certainly benefit family life and add a lot to children's minds. Smartly controlled, they can teach lessons about current affairs and life outside the family, thus helping to bolster children's judgment about people and events. Sometimes they present high-quality entertainment, serving to shape children's tastes and lead family members to enjoy life together, as they should.

It's the excess, the thoughtless overindulgence, that poses problems to parents. And that's what we want to look at here.

Discriminating control

For simplicity's sake, let's use the term *tube-watching* to lump together all uses of the cathode-ray tube at home—commercial and cable television, video games and computer games, surfing the Internet, films via the VCR.

Effective parent leaders team up to control the family's access to the tube. In practice this means they join minds in three high-priority areas:

- to which programs, films, games, and Internet sites the kids will have access;
- how much time will be allotted to this access;
- which programs, films, games, and sites the kids will *not* have access to at all.

What we're talking about here is the power of discernment, that is, assessing programs and allocating time according to the parents' considered judgment. This discernment aims to teach the children over time to *accept what is good, reject what is wrong (or useless), and know the difference.*

In other words, while getting control of the tube, parents work to bolster the children's powers of judgment and self-control. Both parents want to shape up significant lifelong habits: a habit of *not* watching the tube (there is such a thing), a habit of watching only worthwhile programs, and the adult-level stance of seeing time as a resource that shouldn't be frittered away.

So, what standards should parents rely on for choosing

what their children see? The following are found in healthy families:

• We will watch programs and play games that bring us together as a family: sports events, high quality films and entertainment, games that two or more can play.

• We will watch programs and use sites that teach us something and thus strengthen our judgment: news, documentaries, special programs about current events.

• We will not watch programs or play games or access sites that treat human beings as objects. This means a) no pornography (which treats women as objects), b) no gratuitous violence (no practice in killing people for fun), c) no portrayals of characters, especially children, treating others with coarse language or disrespect.

• We will not permit children to watch the tube or play games alone to excess—to the extent that they're wasting precious hours that could otherwise go into healthy pursuits such as sports or reading. We won't let children use the tube in such a way that they draw themselves away from family life.

In short, Dad and Mom assert that the tube will be used only when it promotes family life or serves to build the children's judgment. Any use that strays outside these broad areas is probably negative, or at best a waste of time, and so the screen stays blank.

How can you make a judgment call about a specific program's worth, or whether kids are spending too much time with a game?

The best rule of thumb is this: If you feel uneasy or begin to have reservations, then chances are the line has been crossed already. If a show or game strikes you as too violent, then it probably is. If your son seems to be spending too much time with a video game, he probably is. Your uneasiness is a signal;

it's time to act. Enough is enough. Turn the tube off and point the kids to other recreation that firms up their growing bodies and minds.

This whole area of parental tube-control underscores that iron principle of parental leadership that we've seen before: *Don't let uncertainty lead to inaction.* In any given family-life situation, you may be unsure whether a given decision is right, but you should have no doubts about your right to make a decision in the first place, and to make it stick. Your rights come with the job. When you act for your children's welfare, your right to make and impose a decision should remain unquestioned.

Don't be too concerned about mistakes here, either. Years from now, your children will only dimly remember your mistakes. What they will hold in heartfelt memory all their lives is your loving leadership.

Strengthening your resolve

When you exert yourself to control the tube, keeping its use to a discerning minimum, you'll find this takes time, effort, and sometimes an iron will. It's a tough task, which is why so many parents just give in. You have to spend more time with your children, which means you watch far less TV yourself. You have to struggle to master the kids' resistance to your decisions, wrangling with their pleas and arguments. All this extra work and vexation can wear away at your will.

To stick with the job, you should remind yourself now and then just why, for the children's sake, you must get the upper hand over your electronic rivals. Here are some ideas for you to weigh, some insights to help you steel your resolve for your children's sake:

• Countless psychological studies over the past forty years have shown what a potently convincing force television is to children. (To adults, as well.) Children respect its sheer power. Consequently, if you take action to control the tube—that is, if your own power is greater than that of TV and the computer—then you more deeply win your children's respect. You show you have the power to muscle aside your adversary. In your rivalry with the tube for your children's esteem, you win hands down.

• This respect for your moral authority (leadership in discerning right from wrong) grows especially urgent when your children enter adolescence. Teens with little respect for their parents, especially their father, are strongly attracted to the rock-drugs-sex culture. Their adulation for entertainment figures stems from a vacuum in their longing for leadership. These unfortunate kids have no adults whom they respect enough to imitate. But on the other hand, those teens who deeply respect both parents remain virtually unmoved by the adolescent culture. Like other adolescents, they enjoy much of the music and embrace some of the fashions, but they don't *believe in* the culture—they're not sucked into it heart and soul—and sooner or later they outgrow it. In one way or another, they esteem and thus unconsciously imitate their powerfully confident parents and, as a result, internalize their values.

• Remember this important fact: for children, seeing is believing. Children today have almost no exposure to the realities of grown-up life, and they don't come into the world with sound judgment. So they naturally soak up what they see. They tend to believe what adults set before them in a powerful way. Now, think what your kids witness repeatedly on most tube programming. They spend hours in a frantic, glamorously attractive, make-believe universe where entertainers substitute for heroes, where "problems" are solved without effort and often violently, where commercials flatter them with pseudo-promises of joy, where people (adults and children) address each other with sass and coarse humor, where anything—anything at all—may be done for a laugh. What on earth does any of this have to do with grown-up reality, or with your family life, or what you want your children to become?

- Think, too, what they do *not* witness on the tube. They see no form of work except entertainment and a grotesque caricature of law enforcement. They see no one actually working, praying, or reading. (Have you ever seen anyone on TV reading a book?) They see no old people or clergy or members of minorities except as clownish cartoon-like figures. They never see any "boring" activities either, such as patient labor, careful planning, steady learning through trial and error, quiet but meaningful discussions, the whole array of steady achievements, large and small, that are the stuff of real grown-up life. In fact, television watching is itself so boring that we never see anyone on TV actually watching TV! In the oddball families portrayed on TV sit-coms, everyone is constantly talking and no one watches TV—the exact opposite of many, maybe most, American homes.

- To look at the problem another way, the media attractively display, and thus powerfully endorse, the exact opposite of character strengths. Not level-headed judgment, but emotionalism and bathos. Not real responsibility, but phony and effortless power-grabbing. Not courageous perseverance, but escapism and quick solutions. Not self-mastery, but "shop-till-you-drop" self-indulgence. Not serious, sacrificial concern for others, but a one-note booming message: "Enjoy, enjoy, enjoy . . . for pleasure is what life is all about. . . ."

- Think of time spent with the tube as time away from the family. Remember that kids learn mostly by what they witness, hear, and overhear in family life. None of this is happening—not at all—when your kids sit staring at a screen. You have so much to teach your children about life, love, work, family history, personal honor, integrity, conscience, healthy enjoyment, the adventure of raising a family—the sprawling range of your experienced judgment and principles. You have only a few years to do this, just a tiny window of time. But tube-watching steals that time forever.

• Look closely at your children's bodies and facial expressions while they're staring passively at the tube. Kids' bodies are programmed to be kept in motion; their muscles grow lithe and sinewy through physical action. It's unnatural and positively unhealthy for kids to sit still for hours. Inertia builds flab, not coordinated muscles. And what about their brains? When kids' minds are active, their eyes flit about in constant sweeping motion. They reach out to reality. They scan, search, notice, question, appreciate beauty and courage, make connections between cause and effect, means and ends. But when kids fix their eyes on the tube, they just . . . stare. Their minds float and drift along in a lazy glowing river of sensory stimulation. Is this what your children need?

• Think, too, what else your children could do with all that time, how they might instead be mastering some hobby or recreational skill they could enjoy all their lives. For instance, how many hours do they spend watching or listening to music? What if they spent that same time learning to play an instrument? If they took up the guitar as youngsters and put those same hours into steady practice, they could master the instrument by the time they're in high school. They could empower themselves with a musical skill that would bring lifelong enjoyment, real recreation (re-creating their powers), and delight to the families they'll later form. But what good will hours of cartoons and reruns do for them twenty years from now—or next week, or even tomorrow?

• If just one hour of daily tube-watching went instead into reading, what would happen? Consider this: Suppose your children read thirty pages an hour and did this for only one hour a day, the time devoted to two blathering sit-coms or a few cartoons. This would add up to three or four books a month, about forty books a year, around two hundred substantial books over five years. By any standards, a real accomplishment.

One final thought that might help you stoke your ambition for your children: If your children watch little TV, they may someday be on it.

Think about it. Aside from professional entertainers and the sundry oddballs who bare their woes on talk shows, who are the normal people most often interviewed on TV? They are, of course, people of accomplishment, people who make things happen in significant adult affairs. Do you want your children to become this sort of people? Then here is a fact of life you should pass on to them: People who watch a lot of television almost never appear on television—whereas people who appear on television almost never watch it.

Practical tips

Here are some ideas for getting television and the other electronic media under sensible control:

• Have only one television in the house. A single port of entry is easier to monitor. If you think your family needs a second TV, it shouldn't be in any child's bedroom. Some parents make the mistake of letting children's rooms fill up with a panoply of entertainment gadgets—then wonder why the kids are distracted from homework and pull themselves apart from family life. Effective fathers and mothers see kids' rooms as places exclusively for homework, reading, conversation and quiet play with siblings, and much-needed sleep. Experienced parents will tell you: the more kids' bedrooms resemble yuppie apartments, the more the kids withdraw from the family.

• When children are small, parents pre-select which shows and films will be watched, and when. As the kids grow, they can offer suggestions, but the parents decide matters in final form. Here, as elsewhere in family life, "input" is welcome but it doesn't lead to children's control. The parents are in charge of the house, period. If one parent is unsure about a selection, he or she puts off a decision until consulting with the other.

• Parents establish a firm policy: If children are squabbling over a game or program, they get one warning to cease and desist. If wrangling continues, the tube is shut off at once. The kids will watch in peace or they won't watch at all.

• In cases where parents meet with strong resistance, they resort to more physical control of the tube. This can be done with a small padlock of the type used on suitcases. This little lock fits neatly through one of the holes on the prongs of the television's plug. When the lock is secure on the plug, its prongs can't fit into an electrical outlet. The TV is out of commission until Dad or Mom removes the lock. And they won't remove the lock until their terms are met.

• Sometimes more drastic action is called for—when use of the TV is out of control and the kids seem virtually addicted to it, or, worst of all, they're sneaking TV or the Internet in defiance of their parents. In these cases, parents need to reassert their authority by putting the television or computer out of commission for a set time. Six weeks seems to work best; most habits, it seems, can be formed or undone within six weeks' time. So the parents put the TV or video games or computer in a closet or just seal up the plug with sticky tape, which is almost impossible to remove without cutting. For six weeks, the whole family goes "cold turkey," and during that time they all discover (or rediscover) reading, homework, conversation, games, sports. At the end of six weeks, the parents can reintroduce the tube but strictly on their own terms. By that time, the kids know Dad and Mom mean business. Parents who've resorted to this tactic will tell you it works.

Critical judgment of films and television

Preteens and teenagers need guidance from their parents to form intelligent, critical judgments about the world they live in, especially the world of ideas. Otherwise, they are easily swayed by emotional appeals, propaganda, and commercial or ideological clap-trap. They need leadership to distinguish the good, the true, and the beautiful from whatever is evil, false, and sordid. In sheer self-defense, they should recognize (or at least suspect) when someone is trying to sell them something, especially a false impression or idea.

A critical mind is not a griping mind. Criticism does not mean complaint. It really means a habit of asking active, probing questions to get at the truth and reasonableness of what's put before us—along with the motives of those presenting it. Critical thinking is, in other words, active and intelligent discernment.

What follows below is a list of the kind of questions a savvy, critical viewer would ask of films and television programs. Forming a habit of asking these questions would lead your teens to become critical thinkers, not passive absorbers of sensations and attitudes and ideas, many of which undercut your moral principles. Bear in mind that many teens like to argue for argument's sake and to expose phoniness of all types. So channel this natural love for disputation toward a more critical analysis of the media. Lead them to have good taste and to "know rubbish when they see it."

Here are the questions you and they should ask:

• What is the artistic merit, if any, of this presentation? Is it just meaningless escapist entertainment, a way to pass time without making any change for the better in us? Or is it art—a means to grow in appreciation for beauty, human goodness, and nobility?

• Does the show or film promote materialism, the life-outlook that man is just a beast? Does it treat people as objects by promoting pornography, gratuitous violence, coarseness, and vulgarity? What *emotional responses* does it seek to stimulate—coarse pleasure (including vengeance) at seeing people hurt, dominated, seduced, ridiculed, humiliated? Or, on the other hand, does it lead people to be moved by depiction of noble ideals and sacrificial love (as in, for instance, the classic film *Casablanca*)?

• When a "celebrity" appears on TV, what is he or she celebrated *for*? What has he or she actually accomplished to deserve anyone's serious attention? Is the fame really justified or just artificially contrived? (The American historian Daniel Boorstin said a "celebrity" is someone who's famous for being famous.) Given that TV is essentially a commercial medium, what is the "celebrity" trying to sell? (In other words, follow the money.)

• Would I want this "celebrity" as a guest in my house for a week? Would I want him or her as an in-law? Then why welcome this person as a "guest" in the home via TV?

• When watching an ad: How much or how little is being said about the product and its merits, and how much is claimed about its effects on the buyer? What's being *promised* here—comfort, sensual pleasure, convenience, flattery, social acceptance, or superiority? How many times is the name of the product repeated (count them up), and why? Is price mentioned? Why not?

• How realistic or phony is this show's presentation of life? Does it show people who read, work, pray, plan carefully, sit and think, solve problems without resort to trickery or violence?

• How often does the show have a visual or auditory "event" occur—that is, a swift change of camera angle or sudden noise—to keep the viewer's attention and avoid his drifting away, from boredom? In cartoons and most ads, it's once a second or less. In regular programs, once every three or four seconds. In public-TV interviews, once every eleven seconds. What does this say about the producer's assessment of his viewers' maturity and attention span?

• It is said that most TV shows are aimed at the intelligence level of a twelve-year-old, and that most "action" movies are aimed at sixteen-year-old males. Do these generalizations seem reasonably accurate? Why?

* * *

The flitting images and gadgets and "personalities" of the media are a big part of our culture. (Look in your newspaper's daily crossword puzzle and note how many items refer to shows, movies, and celebrities.) So if your children don't watch much TV or fritter hours away in the latest computer games, they may feel out of touch with kids their age, a little different from their neighbors. This is a problem, sort of.

But think of it this way. All in all, it's not a bad thing for your children to get used to living a little bit different from the crowd, especially in moral matters. Where could the crowd lead them if they're afraid to be different?

It is absolutely certain, have no doubt about it, that your children will one day be pressed by others their age to try drugs, get wasted on beer, see sex as a naughty but normal teenage recreation, and all because "everybody else is doing it."

Parents have to realize that "no" is as much a loving word as "yes." And kids can't say "no" to themselves if they've hardly ever heard it from their parents. Loving parental denial leads to self-denial, and kids can't start shaping up this power from scratch at age thirteen. They are powerless to "say no to drugs" if they're used to having peer-pressures whipsaw and dominate their moral choices. Bumper stickers are no substitute for a conscience.

So there's a payoff later for your efforts. But you don't have to wait long for other benefits to spring up in your family. When both parents get the media under smart control, some wonderful things start happening at home.

You have hours more time each week to learn the ins and outs of your children's minds and let them know yours. Your children pay much more attention to you.

Your authority is enhanced and your kids respect you more deeply. This, as we've seen, is crucial to everything you have to teach them.

Family life centers on conversation, reading, sports, games, hobbies, and work—the "natural" life in families for centuries.

Dinner time becomes a prolonged get-together—nobody's in a hurry to go anywhere.

If you have lots of books around the house, the kids will read them. They'll turn into readers. (Young people who have read a lot since childhood consistently ace the verbal section of the SATs.)

The kids take up musical skills and hobbies that can enrich them all their lives.

Increased activity sheds flab and puts the children in better physical shape. Think ahead: If young people get in good shape by the time they're sixteen, they'll probably stay that way till their mid-forties or later. This enhances their health, their social lives, their marriages, and even their careers. No matter how you look at it, soft and pudgy couch-potatoes are at a competitive disadvantage in the workplace. Unfair, certainly, but true.

Kids have even been known to trudge off and do their homework out of sheer boredom. And since they have few choices but to work, they tend to stick with it till it's finished and done right. They earn better grades in school.

All in all, instead of bombarding their nerve endings with carnival-like noise and jolting sensations, the kids direct their minds into reading, expressive talk, attentive listening, and stretches of benign silence—and they begin to think.

ISSUES FOR REFLECTION AND DISCUSSION

(1) Please comment on this: Before the invention of television, Mom gave her children some subtle signals each day that she was in charge of things. When she had to turn away from a child to handle something for a few minutes, she told her youngster to crayon a picture or play a game or do a puzzle. If the child demurred, or returned again a couple of times for Mom's attention, the mother took action to assert her will. In an affectionate but clear voice, she insisted, "I said to fill in that page with crayons, honey. Now go do it, please, and don't interrupt me until I'm ready." This happened several times a day, and each incident reinforced her loving authority in the home.

Today, in contrast, the TV often acts as a babysitter. When Mom needs to do something else, she can plop the child in front of a screen to be entranced for a spell while she goes about her other business.

But this babysitting function of TV has a subtle side effect. Children are missing these daily signals about who's "boss" in the family. In other words, there's a leveling effect at work: Mom seems more of an equal, not someone who's clearly in control.

How is this phenomenon related to the chapter's discussion about parents' enhanced authority when they, not the children, control use of the tube?

(2) It's been said that television isn't an entertainment medium; it's really a commercial medium. It's main purpose is to sell.

For children, "seeing is believing." So what effect does it have on children to be exposed to a constant barrage of flattering, promise-filled advertising?

(3) Parents who won't allow smut and other coarse material into their home are really acting to teach their values to their children. Their purpose is not to shield the kids from this material, for this is impossible. Children can easily access it elsewhere—in neighbors' homes, for instance. What parents are really doing is driving home their moral convictions, drawing the line between right and wrong. The kids may later do wrong, of course, but what's important is that they *know* it's wrong. And this they learn at home, and for keeps.

How does this stance relate to our discussion about the power of "We . . ."? How does it affect children, long-term, to hear, "Other families allow violence and porn into their homes, but *we* don't . . ."?

(4) It's been noted that successful professional people tend to treat work-related problems as if they were puzzles—that is, not as repulsive hassles but rather as interesting challenges to their powers. There's a confidence and even playfulness in their approach to problem solving. What does tube-watching do, if anything, to enhance this sporting approach to problem solving? On the other hand, what about sports, chess, board games, logic puzzles, hobbies, homework, reading—the whole range of challenging activities that youngsters delight in when the tube is left blank?

(5) For adults, a hobby has healthy long-range benefits. From time to time, it seems, busy adults need some activity where they pull back from life's stresses and concentrate

their powers on something unimportant—that is, unimportant to anyone but themselves. A hobby serves, as it were, as a way by which grown-ups return once again to the delights they knew in childhood, where work and play were one. Moreover, a hobby often passes on from parents to children, thus binding them in a common interest for years. And finally, a hobby gives older adults something to look forward to in retirement; retirees who never cultivated hobby interests grow stifled by boredom.

It's said, too, that among the happiest people we meet are those who managed somehow to turn their hobby into their life's work.

Fact: Children who watch excess TV and video games do not develop hobbies.

Comment?

(6) Teachers lament that many children today don't seem to know how to listen. Kids interrupt and blurt things out and pay scant attention to what others are saying. They seem clueless that conversation means taking turns. Whenever we converse with someone, we don't just take turns talking; we take turns listening.

How does this present-day problem relate to kids' spending so little time conversing in the family—and so very much time with electronic media that talk *at* them but never *with* them? Or watching sit-coms and other dramas where characters hurl each other frantic lines of machine-gun dialogue?

(7) Please comment on this: One rule of thumb for parents to evaluate a film or show or video game is this: What sort of *emotions* does this arouse in those who watch? Healthy or at least harmless humor? Admiration for virtue and nobility? Vengeance? Shock? Triumphal glee at the humiliation of others? Crude, swinish pleasure?

And what about video games? What emotion is cultivated by gleeful practice in violently killing thousands of
people? Does this type of amusement, like the Roman
gladiatorial games, treat people like objects and coarsen
respect for human life?

CHAPTER EIGHT

Issues of the Heart and Mind

In this chapter we probe into the collective wisdom of veteran parents about some crucial issues. These are special areas that bind the family together in heart and mind.

Directional consensus

Though they may differ in any number of other things, a great husband and wife share one mind and will concerning their children's upbringing. They share the same long-term ideal about their children's future as responsible men and women, and they're determined to work together, no matter what, to make this happen.

Great parents, it seems, hold this truth ever before them: each child has only one mind and one conscience, and therefore needs one direction, and only one, coming from each of the parents. Children raised in a united family learn from infancy that each parent is "the boss." What's more, if asked about it, they'd say (and even complain), "Mom and Dad always stick up for each other. . . ."

Children whose parents work hard at this *directional consensus* grow strong in character more quickly. As young teens and high-schoolers, they cannot play one parent off against the other and then scoot through the gap. (Look around and you'll find families where canny kids and teens manipulate their parents this way.)

Parents who know they can count on each other's support are much more confident as leaders. Knowing you're not alone, knowing you can rely on strong back-up, always bolsters courage and confidence. Children led by united parents know mostly confident, clear direction at home, and so they grow steadily in self-confidence.

As a parent, you should never forget: Confident kids resist drugs. Confident teens resist peer-group pressures. Confident workers go places in business because people like working with them; they receive respect, raises, and promotions. Confident, realistic young people tend to marry wisely and then raise confident children themselves.

Part of our courage in life, it seems, derives from growing up in a loving, supportive family. It springs from the purposeful, affectionate, coordinated direction of mutually supportive parents—a man and woman who are confident in each other.

How can parents work at strengthening this mutual support? Here are some approaches that others have relied on:

• First, set some time apart each week, even just a half hour or so, to talk about each of your children: strengths and shortcomings, personal needs and problems, dealings with siblings, courses of action, what to do next. Sunday morning seems to work best for this sort of family shop-talk. Dad should pay special attention to his wife's judgment in these matters. Almost certainly, she has sharper, more sensitive insight than he. Mothers are gifted this way.

• Second, determine that you will never, ever, oppose or demean each other in front of the children, especially when one of you is correcting a child. If either of you thinks the other is wrong, save the discussion for later and work it out privately.

• Third, and related to the above, don't ever carry on a heated quarrel in front of the children. You can voice a difference of opinion or even an argument in the harmless sense. But any sharp clash with a jagged personal edge should be quickly smoothed over by apologies and return to normal affection.

In fact, it's healthy for children to see that sometimes even loving parents will argue but then swiftly reconcile. Everyone has faults and anyone can have a bad day. Spotty flashes of anger flare up in nearly all marriages, but apologies swiftly cover these over. "I'm sorry . . . Please forgive me . . ." is one of the strongest bonds of marriage.

But what is upsetting to children and corrosive to family life is any prolonged and really heated quarrel. The two of you must avoid this at all costs, even that of your pride.

So if you sense that a disagreement is getting out of hand, that an argument is going too far, then have some preestablished signal with each other (like tapping your watch or discreetly giving the "time-out" sign with both hands) which means it's time to drop the subject. That is, you both agree that, no matter how upset you feel at the moment, you'll put off the discussion till later when you're alone. At that time you can thrash things out. But by then, of course, both of you will have calmed down. Whatever it takes, do anything rather than scare the kids.

• Fourth approach: Set a policy that's helpful when your kids are small and extremely important as they enter their teens. It's this: When your children ask your permission in a fairly important matter (sleepovers, camping trips, exemption from house rules, special use of the car, and the like), put off your decision until you've checked with your spouse. And your spouse follows the same deferred-decision policy with respect to you.

Each of you says, "Let me first check with your mom (or dad). . . ." Doing this consistently is important. For one thing, it prevents misunderstandings and arguments between the two of you later. It also reinforces the children's concept of your mutual support; it underscores how you respect each other's judgment. What's more, it keeps wily teens from playing each of you off against the other. And finally, it gives both of you time to reflect about the decision and then set reasonable conditions as you see fit.

Another benefit is that it makes your kids wait for what they want, and this is healthy for them. Your children should not form the corruptive habit, so common among many youngsters and teens today, of expecting *instant gratification*, especially in significant matters. If your children cannot *earn* whatever they want, they can at least *wait* for it. Waiting is healthy for children.

• Finally, what should you do if you find it hard to agree on some specifics of discipline—in house rules, for instance, or types of punishment for serious wrongdoing? You can try several tactics that other parents have relied on.

You can work out a compromise: "OK, we'll try it your way for three months (or whatever) and then we'll try it my way. Let's see how things work out. . . ."

Or, if you have time, seek arbitration. Agree to consult someone you both respect—a good friend, a relative, a teacher, or member of the clergy, anyone with sound judgment and experience in family matters—and agree to abide by his or her advice.

As a last-ditch measure, or if time is pressing, flip a coin! Any decision is better than none at all. As we've noted before, no effective leader ever lets indecision lead to inaction.

No matter what you do, realize that each of you may have to swallow your pride a bit for the sake of presenting a united front to your children. Experience shows that this unity, no matter how arrived at, is far more important than specific tactics. As long as you are together in mind and will, as long as you're both determined to remain united, you can afford to make mistakes along the way. Somehow, in the long run, it works.

Distinctions

One smart father I knew in Washington, D.C., once said this to me:

"I think one of the roles of parents is to teach children the *vocabulary* of right living. That is, kids don't just need to be taught right from wrong; they need specific, concrete words and terms to fasten these concepts into their judgment and keep them there. They need to know the *names* for important ideas. Otherwise, their judgment stays fuzzy and sentimental. They use 'cool,' 'awesome,' 'bad' and other slipshod terms— which are just bubbles of sound surrounding a shapeless, mindless feeling.

"Over several days, I made a list of such words to keep coming back to when teaching and correcting my two boys. It included terms that kids seldom hear these days and only dimly understand. Examples: *honor, integrity, ethics, professionalism, charity, healthy skepticism, self-respect, vanity, etiquette, tact, boorishness, self-indulgence, considerateness, commitment.*

"So, when one of my sons tries to fib his way out of trouble, I refer to his honor and integrity (terms we've discussed before) and he knows what I mean. If his teenage brother tries to weasel out of a promise, we talk in terms of commitment. When I'm checking their homework and see that it's slapdash, I correct them in terms of professionalism—because they know I consider schoolwork a ramp-up to serious professional work. And so on.

"When I was a debater in high school, we used to start each debate with a so-called 'definition of terms.' That is, we'd define each important word in the statement of the resolution. I took this sound idea, which prevents futile semantic arguments, and extended it to teaching my sons mature ethical standards. Once parents teach these terms and what they mean, they can keep referring back to them."

As this wise Dad saw, judgment means, among other powers, the ability to make significant distinctions in life. Children learn these invisible distinctions from their parents and other adults they respect. To list just a few that children need to learn:

- *needs* from *wants*
- *real grown-up life* from *life as depicted on TV*
- *humor* and *wit* from *mean-spirited ridicule*
- the *noble* and *beautiful* from the *sordid* and *squalid*
- *responsible spirit of service* from *immature egoism*
- *healthy skepticism* from *cynicism*
- *heroes* from *"celebrities"* and *entertainers*
- *rule of law* from *personal despotism*
- *courage* from *cowardice*
- *calculated risk-taking* from *recklessness*
- *professionalism* from *sloppiness*
- *reasoned opinions* from *"feelings"*
- *objective* from *subjective*
- *proven fact* and *certain knowledge* from *assumption* and *"impressions"*
- *healthy self-respect* from *vanity* and *pride*
- *reasonable enjoyment* from *self-indulgent excess*
- *love* from *eroticism*
- *courtesy* and *good manners* from *boorishness*
- *tact* from *offensive bluntness*
- *integrity* from *pragmatic disregard for truth and for keeping one's word*
- *honorable competition* from *ruthless ambition*
- *love for family and friends* from *selfishness*

This is a short list, but you get the idea. Try adding to it from your own experience and from details elsewhere in this book: moral discernments that your children need to learn before they're out of their teens.

Learning from mistakes

All conscientious parents want their children to be constructively active. (If the children grow up slothful, they'll be elbowed aside by their competitors.) And smart parents know that active people, youngsters as well as adults, make mistakes. Only the bone-lazy commit few active blunders in life, but they fall headlong into the biggest mistakes of all—neglect, bad timing, missed deadlines, lost opportunities.

So if you lead them to be active self-starters, your children will make many mistakes along the way. You expect this and allow for it. You take advantage of your children's mistakes, in home life or school or sports, as a chance to firm up their judgment. So how should you react?

In two ways. . . .

First, judge whether they were honestly trying to do the right thing. Give them credit and sincere praise for their earnest best efforts. Make clear to them, always, that you don't expect perfection or even success; but they must always try. You insist that they try their best to surpass themselves.

Second, teach them a truth about adult life: mistakes are valuable if we learn from them. Sit down and talk with your children, and lead them to think through what happened. . . .

- What were you thinking when you did this? What did you expect to happen?
- What exactly went wrong?
- What was your reaction? What did you think and feel?
- What did people around you say and do? How did your mistake affect them?

- If your mistake caused a problem or offense to someone else, how do you think they feel right now?
- What can you do now to repair this mistake? If you offended someone, even without meaning to, don't you think you should say you're sorry?
- If you're ever in this situation again, what will you do differently? What have you learned?

I once knew a wise father who worked as a professional pilot for a large commercial airline. He told me this: "From what I can see, most serious teenage problems come from flawed judgment, not malice. Even well-intentioned kids get into trouble because they don't know any better.

"We pilots use a flight simulator in our flight training, and for obvious reasons. Better to goof in virtual reality than in a real seven-thirty-seven at thirty-thousand feet. I see my home life as a kind of simulator for my kids' lives as grown-ups. After all, what is training except learning from experience harmlessly? When they make mistakes, as we all do, it's better to do this at home when they're small and damage is minimal. Better small mistakes now than big mistakes later."

He's right. A healthy family is where children can *experience mistakes harmlessly.* Better to correct bad habits and attitudes now, at home, before these lead to lethal blunders—mistakes that can damage their marriages and careers, or even kill them.

So, correct your kids' mistakes now, while they're still relatively harmless, while you still have time .

Culture and life of the mind

How do parents work to empower their children's minds— their judgment and discrimination, especially in working with ideas? Here are some notes of experience:

(1) Put worthwhile books into their hands, read aloud to them, and encourage them to read on their own. Make reading aloud a part of your family life. Let them form a power and delight of interacting with the written word. The genre of the reading is not so important (adventure stories, biographies, narrative history, mysteries, fantasy), as long as the books are the best in that genre. (Ask for recommendations from knowledgeable people who share your principles.) Later, when they meet excellent literary works, they will recognize this high quality because they'll have a framework for comparison with the works they read as children.

(2) Encourage children (especially after age eleven) to form opinions, but to base these on facts and reasons, not "impressions" or "feelings." Ask, "What makes you *think* so?" and "What do you *think* about that?"—not "How do you *feel* about that?"

(3) Related to this: Lead your children to distinguish between informational questions and speculative ones. When they're asked a "Why" question, they should take risks by making intelligent guesses. They shouldn't shrink back from brainwork through mental sloth or fear of making a mistake. When asked a thought-provoking question in school or at home, intellectually lazy kids will just shrug and blurt out, "I don't know." What they really mean is, of course, "I don't know, and I don't *care* that I don't know." Explain to your children: One sign of an active mind is to try to *account* for things, even just with sensible guesses that we call "speculation." It's no disgrace not to know something, but it is a fault if you just stop there—if you don't care that you don't know and refuse to make an intelligent guess. People who take thoughtful risks go places in life.

(4) If possible, read or scan the same books they're assigned in school. Lead them to think through each book, judge it, ask questions about the author's intent. Put stress on the author's

thought, not just what happens in the book. Lead the kids to see the *person* behind the written word (which is perhaps the most important key to critical reading).

(5) Check their homework, and read it aloud to them—or get them to read it aloud to you. Press them above all to be clear, to put themselves in the place of their reader. Not everyone can write elegantly, but anyone can at least make his meaning understandable. See their written work as a ramp-up to later professional excellence.

(6) When they're about to tackle heavy homework assignments, teach them a truth about life: *the first fifteen minutes are the hardest*—that is, concentrate hard at the very beginning, the toughest part, and momentum carries you forward. As the old maxim puts it, "Well begun is half done."

(7) Read stories aloud into family life; long car trips are a good occasion for this. Younger kids ask questions about words and story developments that they don't yet understand, and your answers subtly lead them to respect your judgment. Reading aloud like this—which is, after all, a kind of service—becomes part of the family's whole formational strategy: leading the children from self to others.

(8) Leave the TV screen blank and press your children to enjoy puzzles, word games, board games, crosswords, spelling matches. Form in them a healthy attitude for life: to see problems as puzzles, challenges to their powers, not just hassles to be endured.

(9) Comment on contemporary news events, especially during dinner or after watching or listening to the news. But don't make dogmas out of your opinions; the children can disagree with you as long as they have reasons for their judgments. Respect their freedom of opinion. And if you must criticize people in public life, be sure to distinguish between the person and the fault: we "hate the sin but love the sinner." We deplore wrongdoing, but we bear no personal ill will toward anyone.

(10) Sing songs together. Play high quality music (of whatever type) in the home and while driving.

(11) If the family is planning a trip, let the older kids consult maps to plan out and suggest possible routes. If the trip includes historical sites, let the kids read about them ahead of time.

(12) For family birthday celebrations, encourage the children to contribute some personal gifts of their own devising: a poem, a song, a homemade birthday card.

(13) In high-school years, encourage several things: join debate or newspaper clubs, master at least one foreign language (four years of study), try for competence (at least) in one team sport and one individual sport—such as tennis, golf, squash, handball, track, martial arts—which can be enjoyed all one's life and thus keep each child in good physical shape through adulthood.

(14) Remember, as Plutarch said, "The mind is not a vessel to be filled; it is a fire to be lit." The object of your work in forming children's judgment is not that the kids have a large data base of information; it is, rather, that they grow to form a love and respect for learning, for intellectual and artistic accomplishment.

(15) When they're teens, press them to read good quality newspapers and magazines, and form habits of asking themselves certain critical questions—

- Who is this person who's speaking (writing) to me?
- What does this person want from me? What am I expected to believe, or do, or buy?
- Are this person's principles the same as mine? Do we share the same values? Is he or she materialistic? How can I tell?
- When a statement is made, what is the factual basis for it? How do we know that it is true, or at least a reasonable conclusion? Are we dealing here with facts or with assumptions—and if assumptions, how reasonable are they?

- How does the questionable statement square with what I have been taught by my parents and other adults whom I respect?

Honor and integrity

Honor. In the context of youngsters' upbringing, the term isn't heard much these days, even though it lies at the core of people's conscience and sense of commitment. Personal honor is one of the most vital lessons parents impart to their children.

Let's say something here about lying.

Nearly all children will blurt out a falsehood to wiggle out of blame and punishment. At least they will try. Lying is one of the two defenses children rely on to thwart adult power; the other, of course, is weeping, bursting into tears.

Certainly, you must never let your youngsters get away with lying, but you should distinguish between a spontaneous on-the-spot fib and a cold-blooded, deliberate falsehood. A purposeful lie is much more serious. It's like the crime of perjury, and, like lying under oath, it's flatly unacceptable. Your children must learn that it's one thing to *lie*—but it's another to *be a liar.*

To live as a liar is to discard personal honor, the trust that people extend to us, and this is an enormous loss. Parents need to hammer this lesson into each child's conscience, and for keeps. Because a commitment to personal honor has lifelong consequences, teaching it relentlessly is one of parents' top-priority duties.

Many great parents rely on the following practice to drive the lesson home, starting when the kids are old enough to understand, around age five: When they suspect their youngster is lying, especially in a fairly serious matter, they say this: "Go to your room and think this over seriously. When you come out, tell me the truth *on your honor.* Whatever you say then, I will believe it—because you're on your honor. . . . And heaven help you if you refuse, on your honor, to tell the truth!"

Children from families with this practice will nearly always tell the truth. Early on, the kids learn that their parents absolutely must be able to trust them; and that, if they lie while on their honor, they do immense damage to that bond between you and them. If they betray your trust by sticking with a lie under honor, and you find out about it later, then you should treat it as a felony (as we saw earlier) and punish severely— with strong, unforgettable explanation about the utter importance of personal trust. Kids who experience this treatment almost never repeat the mistake.

On the other hand, if they admit on their honor that they had fibbed, then just give them some minor, slap-on-the-wrist punishment, but praise them lavishly for having the courage to tell the truth. Welcome them quickly back into your good graces and complete trust. They've earned it, and they've learned a lifelong lesson.

If you live this policy when your children are small, you'll have few problems with openness when they enter adolescence. You may even have no problems at all. By that time, your children will know what you mean when you tell them you trust their integrity. They'll know what the word means.

You can cultivate your children's sense of personal honor and healthy self-respect by occasionally explaining *integrity.*

In adult society, and especially in the workplace, personal integrity ranks higher than any other esteemed trait. Consistently, employers rank integrity as the number one characteristic they demand and expect of their workers; they see it as more important than talent or skills or credentials. Responsible, mature adults know this, of course, but youngsters do not.

What's more, a lack of personal integrity seems to lie behind many marital problems and break-ups. Spouses stop trusting each other, and in time they fall out of love.

Given this nearly universal agreement about integrity, it's puzzling why so many parents fail even to mention the word at home, much less teach what it means.

So, what does it mean? How can you explain integrity to your children?

Try this: The word is related to other terms we use—*integer, integrate, disintegrate*—all centering somehow on unity and wholeness. *Integrity means unity of intention, word, and action.* A person with integrity says what he means, means what he says, and keeps his word. That is, he tells the truth and he keeps his promises. He takes his honor and commitments seriously, sometimes to the point of courageous sacrifice. Integrity is honor put into action.

A moment ago, we saw a way to handle children's attempts to lie, reinforcing their concept of personal honor. Here are some other suggestions.

As much as possible, teach your children this life lesson: Don't make promises lightly, but if you make them, you're obligated to keep your word. If out-of-control circumstances keep you from honoring your promises, then you owe the offended party an immediate, sincere apology. People's respect for your word, your integrity, depends hugely on your *commitment to keep your commitments.*

This is the way honorable, responsible adults live. And this is what your children must learn and live by.

Related to this: Advise them (especially older ones and teens) to form a useful policy in their social dealings with peers, a policy widely found among sensible, savvy adults. It's this: When others urge us to do something, especially if we have even mild misgivings about it, we shouldn't reflexively rush to commit ourselves. Instead, the smart thing is to say, "Let me think about it for a while and get back to you." Doing this gives us room to think things over and, if necessary, get sound advice. It's is a sensible approach that can save us a lot of trouble. After all, whenever we're about give away anything valuable, we all need to think carefully about consequences—and for us our given word is one of our most valuable possessions.

Moreover, try to turn some rules of the home into occasions where kids, older ones especially, obligate themselves through their given word. For instance, rather than impose a curfew on your teens to return from a dance, negotiate with them about a reasonable hour. (The word "reasonable" goes very far with teenagers.) Then exact from them a promise to return at that time. From that point on, their responsibility is not just to obey your curfew but rather to keep their word, to hold up their end of the agreement.

As much as you can, try to treat your teenage children as responsible adults. When you apply this tactic—that is, exacting promises rather than obedience—you're giving them a sense of the way responsible adults do business. Outside of the military, an employee doesn't really "obey" his boss so much as he honors his business commitments. He makes certain promises to his company, spelled out in his job description and contract, and he labors to keep his word. This is the way professional life works.

Other approaches along this line with younger kids: You ask them, "When will you start your chores this evening? . . . Is that a promise?" "Will you call from the game if you're going to be late? . . . You promise?" "Have you done your best on your homework? Do I have your word on that?"

If the kids fail to follow through, then they're committing two mistakes: the misdeed itself and their failure to keep their promise. Clearly, it's the word-breaking that's more serious to you, and this is what you come down on.

In the same way, you teach integrity in the areas of accepting invitations and keeping appointments. Spoiled children accept invitations with thoughtless impulse, and then feel free to ignore them if something more enticing pops up. What's more, they see no reason to apologize for this word-breaking and will even give the offended party a phony excuse.

Don't let your kids get away with this. We can be whimsically casual about many things, but not our given word. So you maintain a flat rule in the house: Don't accept any invitations until you've first checked with your parents. And then once you've accepted, you're obligated to be there, period.

The same holds true for appointments, say, with music lessons, visits to the doctor or dentist, sports practices. Your children must show up every time, and on time, and with any equipment they need. An appointment is really a promise, and we keep our promises.

If your children plead to undertake some long-term activity—guitar lessons, karate, Scouting, buying and caring for a pet, delivering newspapers, and the like—you first make them think the matter through and then commit themselves for a reasonable trial period. They promise to stick with the activity for, say, a year or six months, and they may not quit before that time even if they tire of it. A promise is a promise. In this way, they learn that our given word is more important than our convenience or whimsical wishes. This is the way responsible grown-ups live. Routinely we put commitment ahead of comfort, especially in the greatest of all commitments: marriage.

Finally, there should be no falsehood in your family. You should never lie to your children.

This doesn't mean the kids need to know everything that passes between you and your spouse, or any confidential matters between you and your other children. The "need-to-know" principle applies as much in family life as in business.

As people of integrity, you and your spouse never withhold information from someone who has a clear right to it, but that doesn't mean you're obligated to share everything with the children. It's your call where to draw the line here. In any event, do not tell falsehoods. Whatever the kids hear from you must be the truth.

The one apparent exception to this is, of course, Santa Claus. The story of Santa is false only in the sense that any fictional literary work is false. It's a game, a harmless make-believe, not a lie. Our Santa Claus fable serves the same purpose as the fairy tales we read at bedtime—to bring delight to children and to exemplify, indeed glorify, kindness and generosity.

Your ongoing effort to teach integrity has long-term consequences for your children's lives. Their success in business and social life will depend on it. And they'll be solidly prepared for life's greatest commitment: a happy, stable, permanent marriage.

Signs of progress

How can you tell that you are making progress with your children, that they are really growing up? Like this: in fits and starts, little by little, you see signs of the following breakthroughs. . . .

— They're aware of the rights and feelings of others, and act this way.

— They have a habit of work. In family life, they are conscious of being needed. That is, they grasp the meaning of *responsibility*: if we don't do our duty, someone else will suffer.

— They live like producers, not just consumers.

— They can take care of others, and want to.

— Most of the time, in a host of situations, they do the right thing without being told.

147

— When they've done wrong, they know it, and they apologize. They accept the apologies of others, and they forget as well as forgive.

— They say, and mean, *please* and *thank you* and *I'm sorry*.

— They keep their promises. They will endure hardship rather than break their word.

— Most of their blunders come not from ill will or selfishness, but rather from lack of experience. By and large, they try to do the right thing.

— They refrain from whatever would disgrace their family.

— They choose friends of upright character.

— Their prayers are addressed to God as a person. They see sin as a rupture of their personal friendship with God, an offense calling for apology and amendment. They see the Church as an extension of their family—worthy of their love and loyalty, no matter what.

— People outside your family—friends and neighbors—compliment you for the quality of your children's character.

One final point. The last item above mentions how receiving compliments from neighbors and friends is a hopeful sign for parents.

Very often these compliments come as a surprise to parents of teens and preteens, largely because of this fact: *The last place where well-brought-up kids behave rightly is at home.* Outside the home, while babysitting or working part-time jobs or just visiting friends, the kids live the courtesy and virtues (albeit imperfectly) that their parents have taught so patiently for years. But at home . . . !

When parents hear these compliments, they often silently say to themselves, "Are we talking about the same kids? . . . You should see the mess in our house on Saturday mornings! You should hear the bickering and squabbling, and the countless times we need to correct them!"

Take courage. Remember, there's such a thing as being too close to a problem. If you stand too close to a painting, even a masterpiece, all you see are meaningless blobs and blotches of color; to see the work in all its beauty, you must stand back at some distance and then look at the whole.

So, too, with your family life. Your friends don't need to see the tangles of your family life, for in the long run these things don't really matter. What they see more clearly than you, because they see from a distance, is your family life where it really counts—in the conscience and character of your children.

Veteran parents can tell you: Finally, at some point, at long last, the teens begin to behave at home every bit as well as they do outside. That's when you will fully realize what your friends and neighbors have admired all along: You've won.

ISSUES FOR REFLECTION AND DISCUSSION

(1) Please comment on this: When parents routinely check with each other before granting permission to kids, as described above, they act to reinforce each other's authority in the children's eyes. They enhance each other's "reputation" in the family, and this is especially important for Dad's influence because the children see less of him. It seems that children's respect for each parent derives from the parents' respect for each other.

(2) Many parents have found this: When each parent puts the other spouse first, then this takes care of half the job of children's upbringing. In other words, when the kids see that Mom considers Dad the Number One person in the family—and Dad treats Mom as Number One—then most other family lessons fall into place. The kids see

firsthand what married love, and therefore family life, is all about.

This may explain why many "only child" youngsters are not at all spoiled. That is, the parents do not direct most of their attention to the single child; rather, their love toward each other matches, at least, the love each of them shows toward their child. So, even though the youngster has no siblings, he or she still grows up in an environment of devoted, other-directed love.

Comment?

(3) This chapter outlines a list of some distinctions ("invisible realities") that parents must lead children to grasp. Can you cite other distinctions?

(4) It is said that the long and the short of parent leadership is this: "To walk the kids through the giving of self."

Comment?

(5) One of the great benefits of a sound, well-coached athletics program is that it can teach kids integrity, the importance of keeping our word.

In baseball, if a player is tagged out at second base—that is, called out by the umpire—he has to leave the field, no matter how upset he is or even if the umpire made a bad call. Why? Because those are the rules and, more important, the player has obligated himself to follow them.

This is a subtle but important lesson for kids to understand: When we put on a uniform, we *implicitly agree* to play by the rules of the game. In a sense, we give our word.

So when an aggrieved player angrily refuses to leave the field and persists unreasonably to argue with the umpire, even his own teammates will gradually turn on him. His real problem is that he's going back on his implied agreement to abide by the rules, and this is considered dishonorable.

How does this lesson carry forward to life in the business and professional world? How can parents explain the crucial importance of integrity (keeping one's word) in business affairs?

(6) With respect to critical reading: It seems that most of us develop a habit in childhood (mostly from our dealings with school textbooks) of deferring to the "authority" of the written word. If something appears in books or periodicals, we unconsciously assume that it's probably true. (Much the same happens with what we hear on television, though probably less so.)

The key to critical reading—dealing with others' ideas discerningly, even cautiously—seems to come from looking at the *person* behind the writing. In other words, we don't just absorb a faceless, anonymous text but rather question the person who's addressing us—and we wonder what the author is up to, what he or she is trying to move us to see, do, or believe.

How can this habit of "person-related" reading be taught to children, especially older ones?

(7) Many adults who enjoy playing a musical instrument were pressed by their parents to persevere in their lessons and practice sessions. Though they resisted this pressure, sometimes even resented it, they are now grateful that their parents ignored their gripes and empowered them to develop this skill. (Do you know anyone who actually regrets being able to play an instrument?)

How does this dynamic—resisting the children's resistance for the sake of their long-term benefit—pertain to parents' loving leadership in other areas?

CHAPTER NINE

Parents' Wisdom: Forming Children's Judgment

There's a collection of truths about life that each generation hands on to the next as a kind of moral legacy. This life-knowledge goes way beyond skill-instruction or mere factual information, the standard stuff of schools. In a word, it is wisdom. Wisdom is taught and learned mostly at home from the experienced insights and advice of our parents.

These parental life-lessons are reinforced later, not so much in school or college but usually on young peoples' first job, their first real experience with grown-up responsibilities. Later still, these lessons really hit home during the first few years of marriage. "Dad and Mom were right . . ."—this is what young people come to see.

Here's a real-life example of this shrewd lesson-giving in action:

I was once talking with a mother about how young adults of marriageable age need to size up the character of a prospective spouse and how hard this is to do when, as they say, love is blind.

She told me this story: "When I was leaving home to start college, my Dad gave me one of the best pieces of advice I ever received. He said that someday I'd fall in love with a young man and seriously consider marrying him. At that time, he warned, I'd probably find it hard to be objective about the man, to read deeply inside his character. So this was his advice—Look closely at the way this man treats his grown brothers and sisters. Is he affectionate with them? Does he like and respect them? Does he remember their birthdays? Is he proud of them, glad to be around them? Does he stay in touch with them? . . . Or, on the other hand, is he indifferent to them? Does he quarrel with them, bear grudges, keep them at a distance? . . . Chances are (he said), this is a preview of the way he will treat his spouse: The way a man treats his siblings is the same way he'll treat his wife.

"I took my Dad's advice. I went through several brief relationships until I met a young man who was proud of his own family and affectionate with all of them. He's now my husband."

So, what are some of these important insights about people and interpersonal dealings that parents need to teach their children, especially from early adolescence? Here are some I have culled from the experience of wise parents, life-lessons that can firm up your children's judgment and moral sensibilities:

(1) You can tell a lot about people's quality by . . .
— the kind of friends they choose
— the heroes they admire
— the vigor and joy that they put into their work
— how they treat their parents and siblings
— how kind they are to other people's children
— the measure of affectionate respect they earn from their children
— how they treat people over them and under them at work
— whether they're friendly toward everyone, or just to people they can use
— how competently and considerately they drive a car
— what they talk most often about: whatever's closest to their hearts.

(2) Everybody is a package deal, a mixture of good qualities and personal shortcomings. Consequently, if you look for defects in people, you'll always find them. People who habitually harp about people's faults are really, deep down, unhappy with themselves.

(3) When people complain too much about some fault in others, they're unwittingly revealing their own dominant flaw. Inert people are annoyed by others' laziness. Inconsiderate people are irked by perceived rudeness. Disorganized people can't stand others' messes. People who are casual about the truth are quick to assume that others are liars. Phonies see hypocrisy all around them. Gossips fear betrayal of their confidence. Control freaks gripe about "tyranny."

(4) The whole world, it seems, is divided into two types of people. On one side are the vast majority: normal, decent people who seek goodness, truth, and beauty in life. These delights they find in family, friendship, work, leisure, sports, art, nature, and other healthy human interests. On the other side are the minority: those who single-mindedly chase after *power* above all else. They devote themselves to imposing their will by bullying or manipulating others. They value people only for their usefulness; they treat words as weapons; they break promises when it suits them; they lust for gossip and traffic in it; they promote their interests above anyone else's rights; they're preoccupied, even obsessed, with the architectonics of control. Avoid these people. Try not to work under them. Above all, never vote them into public office.

(5) An ideology is the lust for power disguised as a noble ideal.

(6) Our moral principles are our compass in life, and they simplify life's choices. To people without principles, life is always complicated.

(7) We should always maintain an open mind, but not so open that our brains fall out.

(8) Fear in the face of adversity is nothing to be ashamed of. In fact, it's a sign of intelligence, for only fools are never afraid. Courage consists of doing our duty in spite of our fears. Do we handle the problem as best we can, relying on God's help . . . or do we just run away?

(9) Self-pity is, at best, a waste of time and psychic energy. It causes "yesterday" to crowd out too much of "today."

(10) Money is just an instrument for the welfare of our loved ones and those in need. And that's all it is.

(11) No matter how old you are, avoid staying out on the street after 1:00 A.M. Look at the news stories and note how much senseless violence rages on the street between midnight and dawn. In the small hours of the morning, a high percentage of people on the street are afflicted with some out-of-control problem; large numbers of them are drunk, drugged, violent, or crazy. If you doubt this, ask any police officer.

(12) You can and should size people up, especially if you do business with them. But be careful about judging people. If you must judge, you're obligated to base your assessment on factual evidence—never just on rumor, gossip, or "general impressions." Everybody has a right to presumption of innocence.

(13) Real friendship is based on mutual respect, not merely feelings. The deepest, most long-lasting friendships arise among people who greatly respect each other's character.

(14) A real friend is someone you don't have to pretend with, and couldn't even if you wanted to. A real friend extends you understanding, sympathy, and time.

(15) Apart from our family and religious principles, close friends are our greatest help in making important decisions.

(16) One sign of deep friendship: You and your friend can share silence together, as when you drive somewhere sitting side by side. Silences aren't awkward. Only superficial acquaintances feel a need to fill time with chatter.

(17) Watch out for so-called friends who offer to lie for you in order to get you out of trouble. If they'd lie *for* you, they'd also lie *to* you. People are never dishonest in just one part of their lives.

(18) Only fools, sneaks, and cowards put faith in gossip.

(19) Cynics are people who habitually mistrust the honesty and good intentions of others. Very often they do this to justify their own nastiness; that is, they project onto others the mean spirit inside themselves. Sometimes young people will affect a cynical attitude because they think it implies wide experience with life, something which they really lack. If you scratch a cynic, you'll usually find an insecure naïf.

(20) When you're thinking seriously of marrying someone, pay close attention to how that person treats his or her own family. It's a preview of things to come.

(21) If you're thinking about marrying someone with some defect that troubles you, don't count on that person's reforming after you're married. This rarely happens. By and large, what you see before marriage is what you get afterwards.

(22) Marriages are healthy when both spouses work to improve themselves, not each other. When spouses try to change each other, the result is trouble. (The obvious exception here is helping a loved one overcome alcohol or other substance abuse; this requires relentless love and professional help.)

(23) Sometimes it requires more wisdom to take good advice than to give it. Responsible adults frequently seek sound advice and generally follow it.

(24) Don't give advice unless you're asked for it, and then keep it brief. Remember, too, when people seek advice from you, what they really want is encouragement.

(25) Deep down, people's greatest need is to feel appreciated. This is true in family life, friendship, and the workplace.

(26) The opposite of love is not hatred, but indifference. In some ways, indifference is more painful than hatred. When

we're indifferent to people, we treat them as though they were mere objects, things of no consequence. Hatred points accusingly at behavior, but indifference directly attacks one's dignity as a person.

(27) Anger almost always arises from some sort of fear, especially fear of losing one's self-esteem. So if you're trying to deal with an angry person, first try to figure out: What is he or she really afraid of?

(28) Never send a letter or memo that you've written in anger. If you do, you'll probably regret it. Hold it for a day or two, look it over calmly, then either revise it or throw it away.

(29) Don't ever put anything in writing that could, in the wrong hands, be damaging or embarrassing to you. Documents tend to take on a life of their own; their circulation is hard, sometimes impossible, to control. This is especially true of e-mails.

(30) Never put your signature to anything without first reading it carefully. If you sign something carelessly, you may wind up needing a lawyer.

(31) Litigation is an extremely serious matter. Only naïve simpletons make impetuous threats to sue. Never threaten litigation unless you've thought matters through, really need to protect your rights, and have consulted with legal counsel.

(32) Confident, considerate people are never afraid to apologize. When you have a quarrel with someone (especially your spouse), be the first to say, "I'm sorry; please forgive me."

(33) If anyone is offended by something you said or did, even if you didn't mean to give offense, say you're sorry anyway. You can always honestly say, "I'm sorry your feelings were hurt."

(34) Good manners are the way we show respect for other people's rights and dignity. Since courtesy shows good judgment and self-control, it wins people's respect. In other

words, when we show respect to others, we gain their respect in turn.

(35) Dress for the job you want, not the one you have. Let your grooming and comportment reflect your self-respect.

(36) When you drive a car, you're directly responsible for the lives and physical safety of passengers and other people on the road. No teenager in our family will drive a car until he or she shows this responsibility in family life. When you keep your room clean, manage your own affairs, control your temper, and otherwise show consideration for others' needs and rights at home, only *then* will you drive—not before.

(37) Don't interrupt people. Be patient with slow talkers; don't finish their sentences for them. If you're a good listener, you'll attract good friends. Notice that people who rise to the top in business are generally good listeners and good explainers.

(38) When you converse with anyone, go out of your way to make eye contact. You show that you're listening and are interested.

(39) Never tell racist, ethnic, or sexist jokes. They're hurtful to people and therefore dishonorable. Besides, they can land you in trouble.

(40) Be nice to people who wait on you or clean up after you: janitors, salespeople, waiters, bus drivers, people behind a counter. Look them in the eye, smile, say "please" and "thank you." They're human beings like you, with dignity and feelings, but they seldom receive the courtesy and kindness they deserve.

(41) Don't preface an invitation by asking, "What are you doing this Friday night?" or "Do you have any plans for Saturday?" or anything of the sort. This puts people on the spot. Leave your friends a way, if they prefer, to decline your invitation gently and diplomatically.

(42) Always be punctual in keeping appointments, even with

light social occasions, even with good friends. If you're unavoidably late, try to call ahead; in any case, offer an apology.

(43) When you're invited to someone's home, try to arrive on the dot, no more than five minutes late. Don't arrive early, though, for your hosts may not yet be ready to receive you.

(44) When you phone someone you don't know well, you should identify yourself to whoever answers the call.

(45) Before launching into a phone conversation, first ask if this is a good time to talk.

(46) When you want to praise someone, make it sincere and brief. If you overdo praise, it sounds phony.

(47) "Thank you" is always an appropriate response to any kind of praise or favor. When you're at a loss for words to respond, just say "thank you" and let it go at that.

(48) Never fail to send a thank-you note immediately for gifts, job interviews, and substantial favors.

(49) Tedium is part of life. Most really important accomplishments in life—moving up in a career, forming a stable family life, mastering some skill—involve stretches of repetitive and apparently non-productive action. Having a great goal or ideal is what turns drudgery into adventure.

(50) Most great adventures in history (including the adventure of raising a family) only seem like one at the beginning and at the end: when we set off enthusiastically, and then when we finally triumph. In between, any adventure often seems like just one darned thing after another. That's why we need to pause once in a while to reset our bearings, rekindle our enthusiasm, and rededicate ourselves to our ideals.

(51) To teens: "Potential" is for youngsters. As you approach eighteen, people increasingly want to know how productively you've used your time. To employers and college admissions officers, the best predictor of future success is past success.

(52) In adolescence, the choices we make and the habits we form have lifelong consequences.

(53) There's no tyranny worse than an inability to control oneself.

(54) Always remember this: When you're a parent some-day, you'll have one chance—and only one—to raise your children right.

(55) Your mother is a great woman. *To daughters*: Your mother is a model for the kind of woman you should grow up to become. *To sons*: If you can manage someday, somehow, to marry a woman who's as great as your mother, you can count your life a success.

(56) *To sons*: Women are more verbally gifted than men. They express their thoughts and feelings more aptly in words, and verbal expression means a lot to them. For this reason, every man must often express his love for his wife in words: "I love you . . . You are everything to me . . . I will never stop loving you. . . ." It's not enough to serve her wordlessly with your deeds, or to assume she knows deep down how much you love her. She needs to *hear the words*.

(57) *To daughters*: Don't let men's cool, self-restrained exterior fool you. Men feel emotions deeply but they're reluctant to express these openly on the surface. There's no point complaining about this: it's just the way adult males are wired. Men express their love mostly in deeds: in their hard self-sacrificing work, their acts of service, their availability, their willingness to endure hardship silently for the sake of their loved ones. Unfortunately, sometimes a wife will mis-takenly see her husband's job as the biggest *obstacle* to his involvement at home; whereas he sees his work as his *single greatest contribution* to his family's welfare. This one gross misunderstanding is responsible for at least half the problems in today's marriages. Lesson: Don't ever underestimate your husband's love, and try hard to see his life of work as

he sees it. Remember, love means mostly compassionate understanding.

(58) When good-willed people are angry with each other, the main causes are threefold: a) misunderstanding caused by miscommunication, b) tight deadlines and other extraneous pressures, c) sheer physical fatigue. Under these circumstances, even saintly people can lose control of their tempers. Remember this when you are married. Be patient with your loved ones, and never let the sun go down on your anger.

(59) One of the strongest bonds in society is that among siblings. Take care of your brothers and sisters. All your life, no matter what happens, you can always count on them.

(60) Love isn't just sweet sentiments. It's the willingness and ability to undergo sacrifice for the welfare and happiness of others. Love turns everyday toil into noble adventure. In a real sense, love makes life—love *is* life.

(61) A shortcut to personal happiness: forget about your ego and give yourself generously to serve the needs of those around you, starting with your family

(62) Hard work without some motivating ideal is just drudgery; but that same hard work, done for some great passionate love, turns into noble sacrifice—and life becomes an adventure.

(63) Our concept of death determines the way we live. For those who see death as the end of everything, life ricochets between reckless pleasure-pursuit and fearful despair. But for those who see this life as preparation for the next—who see themselves watched over by a loving, forgiving, all-powerful Father—life turns into a joyful, fascinating, adventurous comedy.

(64) The real riches in life are family, friends, faith, and a clear conscience. Everything else is gravy.

(65) We should pray as if everything depended on God—and act as if everything depended on us. This is the sure way to a great life.

(66) God commands all of us, "Honor your father and mother." The finest honor and gratitude you children can give to us, your parents, is to adopt our principles and religious values, live by them all your lives, and pass them on to our grandchildren.

ISSUES FOR REFLECTION AND DISCUSSION

(1) Are there any life-lessons above that you'd qualify in some way? How so?

(2) Do any of these life-lessons remind you of things your own parents or grandparents would sometimes say? On what occasions?—Commenting on the news? When recounting their business or social dealings? When you started a social life in high school? When you started working? When you shared a personal problem with them?

Why is it important for teens to understand people more deeply—their ethics, values, motivations, strengths and flaws of character—as they set out to live as adults? If they don't receive these insights at home, where will they learn them? What could happen if they don't?

(3) Notice that some of these life-lessons appear implicitly as moral themes in the greatest works of literature, including foreign works from other cultures and historical eras. What does this tell us about human nature—and why literary studies are called the "humanities"?

And why, do you suppose, these life-lessons are seldom explored in school?

(4) Point number 1 mentions several ways we can read people's character. Can you mention any others?

CHAPTER TEN

Parents' Wisdom: Forming a Great Family

In the preceding chapter, we looked at some words of wise advice that parents pass on to their growing children, insights that form the children's judgment about dealing with people and making their way through life.

Here let's look at the experienced wisdom of parents about family life, the kind of advice parents would pass on to other parents, including their grown children who are starting families of their own. As you know, conscientious young parents have all sorts of questions that cry out for sensible, experienced advice and encouragement. This is normal and natural, and it's been going on for centuries.

A curious thing often happens when young parents, striving to do the right thing with their small children, ask advice from older "veteran" parents. The new fathers and mothers pose questions, usually in great detail and even with some anxiety, about the puzzles and uncertainties that vex them every day: What's age-appropriate? What's normal? What kind of discipline fits a certain crisis situation, and how can you tell? How do you deal with youngsters' sulkiness, wildness, resistance to correction, sibling rivalry, and on and on?

How do the older parents respond? Usually, of course, they reach back into their memory of trial and error and recount in detail what worked with them.

But sometimes, very often in fact, they respond differently: with a mildly dismissive shrug or wave of the hand, a soft smile of recognition and remembrance. They're amused to see once again the minutely detailed concerns that they, too, used to worry about before they learned better. "Don't worry so much about that," they say. "You're worrying too much about nitty-gritty details, things that don't matter much in the long run. You should focus instead on what's really important." Through their years of experience, they've grown to realize what's important and what's not. That is, they have wisdom.

If you asked such veterans (as I have) what they've found to be really important in raising children right, here are some principles they'd pass on to you—the compass-points of family life we've studied in this book:

(1) Don't look for recipes or fixed formulas for raising children; there are none. And don't expect perfection from your spouse, your children, or yourself. Instead, set a realistic ideal for your children as responsible adults, and then strive to work with your spouse toward that ideal in unified parental leadership. Ask each other from time to time: "What do you need from me to be more effective, to feel more lovingly supported, and to have greater peace of mind?"

(2) Be confident of your rightful authority, which comes from your God-given vocation, and insist that your children respect it.

(3) Remind yourself often: you're raising adults, not children.

(4) Give your children time and affection, not money.

(5) When you think of your children's futures, picture their character, not just their careers.

(6) Teach the great character strengths as the points of your compass: sound judgment, a sense of responsibility, courageous perseverance, self-mastery, faith, hope, and charity.

(7) Teach your children, relentlessly, the four great pillars of civilized dealings with others: "please," "thank you," "I'm sorry," and "I give my word. . . ."

(8) Remember, the whole of moral development means

moving from *self* to *others*. Your children will not grow up when they can take care of themselves; they will grow up only when they can take care of others, and want to.

(9) Teach them what real love means: sacrifice, including risk-taking, for the happiness and welfare of others.

(10) Raise your children to be producers, not just consumers. Let them put their powers up against problems to solve them and thus grow in self-confidence. We humans are born to serve, not to shop. Show them that real happiness comes from doing good, not feeling good.

(11) Direct, but don't micromanage, your older children's work; don't do their work for them unless and until they've tried their best. Push for personal best effort, not just results.

(12) Make your children wait for something they want, and if possible make them earn it.

(13) Make your kids feel needed and appreciated; make praise as specific as blame.

(14) Teach your children the meaning of the word "integrity." Integrity is unity of intention, word, and action—that we mean what we say, we say what we mean, and we keep our word.

(15) Trust their integrity, even if you must sometimes mistrust their judgment.

(16) Show them how to recognize materialism when they see it, and to shun it. Materialism is not merely the pursuit of things. It means putting things ahead of people. It leads to *seeing and treating other people as things.*

(17) Keep the media—your rivals—under your discerning control. Permit nothing in your home that offends God, undermines your lessons of right and wrong, and treats other people as mere objects.

(18) Lead them to practice the virtue of charity. Charity does not mean giving away old clothes; it means mostly compassionate understanding. In family life, insist on apologies

and forgiveness. Make your kids let others off the hook, forgive and forget

(19) When you comment about people outside the family, especially in public life (in government or the media), practice charity. Distinguish between the individuals and their faults, even grievous moral flaws. We strive to "hate the sin but love the sinner." That is, we deplore people's wrongdoing but bear them no personal ill will.

(20) Lead kids to learn from their own mistakes and the mistakes of others.

(21) Lead them to be savvy about people's values—that is, people's priorities in life.

(22) Use literature, TV, and movies to teach about people's ideals, achievements, and mistakes.

(23) Teach your children to manage time—that is, to control themselves.

(24) Teach them courtesy and "class": to have eyes for the needs of those around them.

(25) Cultivate family honor, the spirit of "We. . ."

(26) Let your kids know what's expected of them. Make standards and consequences clear.

(27) Listen to your children. That's listen, not obey. Let kids contribute "input" to family life—but in weighty issues, you make the decisions.

(28) Where appropriate, give your children "loving denial"—for "no" is as much a loving word as "yes." If kids don't hear "no" from their parents, they cannot say "no" to themselves. The power of self-control is built from the outside in.

(29) Practice "affectionate assertiveness" in disciplining your children. Correct the fault, not the person; hate the sin, love the sinner. Show your children you love them too much to let them grow up with their faults uncorrected.

(30) Treat punishment as "memorable correction"—that is, action needed now to avert later troubles and sorrow.

(31) Take corrective action without showing disrespect. Respect your children's rights as people.

(32) Explain, but don't argue.

(33) Don't let your ego come ahead of truth or justice; when you've done wrong or gone too far, apologize.

(34) Don't let them infringe on the rights of others. Remember, the way they treat their siblings is an apprenticeship for the way they'll treat spouse, children, colleagues, and others in their lives.

(35) Appeal to the children's sense of fairness and capacity to forgive. Make them apologize, and accept apologies.

(36) Make dinner a sacred time: no arguing or squabbling. Start dinner with a prayer.

(37) Encourage a reasonable level of athletic involvement. Use athletics to inculcate the benefits of sportsmanship and exerting one's best effort and staying in shape. But put first things first. Don't let organized sports conflict unreasonably with dinner time or otherwise wreak havoc in family life. Frantic running around robs the family of time and peace of mind. Sports should energize family members, not exhaust them. If you sense that things are getting out of hand, cut back.

(38) Remind yourself: Busyness is not a virtue. Kids, like adults, occasionally need silence and time to think. They need stretches of time to chat and play and daydream together with brothers and sisters, to know and appreciate each other better as they grow up together.

(39) Don't let teens drive a car until they've really grown up. See maturity as growth in responsibility—that is, active concern for the rights and feelings of others.

(40) Teach them indifference to being "different."

(41) Teach them that beer is not a kind of soft drink with a buzz. Alcohol is a drug, drunkenness is a grave sin, and intemperance often leads to tragedies.

(42) Teach kids to cope with reasonable adversity, not to escape.

(43) Lead your children to treat the opposite sex with respect.

(44) Have faith in later results; see your sacrifices as investment.

(45) Keep your priorities straight: when you're vexed with a problem, ask yourself: "How important will this be a year from now, five years from now, or even next month?"

(46) Beware the temptation to fret overmuch about your children's flaws and shortcomings. Since defects and back-sliding are so annoying, they cause us to exaggerate and over-react, to stress the negative. Take time often to appreciate what's good in your children, the qualities they were born with and the virtues you see growing inside them. Remember, people's greatest need, at all ages, is to be appreciated.

(47) Be affectionate with your children. Do this frequently and on purpose. Listen with your eyes. Make the time to have fun with them; let them see how much you enjoy just being with them. When they're teens, actively seek out chances to talk and laugh with them as "best friends"—late-night talk sessions, lingering over dinner, swapping jokes and reminiscences, going to games and shows with them. All their lives, your children's hearts will return home, to the place where they knew affection.

(48) Remember that your children may forget most of the details of what you teach them, but they will remember what was *important* to you. For most of us, the lifelong voice of conscience is the voice of our parents: God speaking to us through the memory of what our parents lovingly taught us.

(49) When your children leave home for college or beginning their careers, tell them this: Don't forget that God is watching over you with love, as He has since your childhood. Do not offend Him, and do nothing that would betray what

you learned in our family. We will pray for you every day. Remember that God commands all of us, "Honor your father and mother." And the way we honor our parents is this: we adopt their values as our own, live by them all our lives, and then pass them on to our own children as our family's sacred heritage.

(50) Treat your children the way God treats all of us: with high standards, loving protection, great hopes for the future, affectionate understanding, readiness to forgive, and never-failing love.

CHAPTER ELEVEN

Summary: A Composite Picture
of Parent Leaders

Throughout this book, we've looked at the mission and job description of great parents, those valiant men and women who prepare their children to lead a great life. By way of summary, how would we describe these parent leaders in action? How do they carry out the adventure of raising a family? This is what we see:

(1) The husband puts his wife first. In his priorities, her happiness and welfare are his top priority, and his children know this. They know it because he leads them by his own example to love, honor, and obey their mother. If they fail to do this, they answer to him for it. (This is more than half the secret of effective fatherhood: striving to live as a devoted, affectionately supportive husband.)

(2) The wife puts her husband first. Her husband's welfare and happiness come closest to her heart, and the children know this. In countless small ways, she leads the children to honor their dad. She never belittles or contradicts him in front of the children, for this would undercut his authority and lead the children to disrespect him. She deeply appreciates his loving sacrifices, including his long hours of work, and she shows this. She leads the children to see their father as a heroic man—a pattern for each son's manliness and a model for each daughter's later choice of a husband. Besides, she's canny enough to foresee the future; when the children

are adolescents, and too big for her to handle in tight situations, it is Dad who will handle matters more effectively. But this will work only if, by then, the kids have a lifelong habit of respecting their father.

(3) So both parents see themselves as partners in a collective team enterprise. Together they strive to present a united front to the children. They check with each other about decisions, large and small, that affect the children's welfare. They draw on each other's strengths and, in different but complementary ways, they reinforce each other.

(4) They see that all their sacrificial efforts, the rigorous work of parenthood, as an *investment*, not just a vexing hassle. They are investing most of all in the stability and happiness of their children's future marriages, not just their careers. They sense that whatever will make their children great spouses and parents will also lead to success in their careers. Mom and Dad look forward to their later reward, the payback for all their sacrifices: being proud of their grown children and enjoying life with their grandchildren.

(5) They correct their children's faults, not them personally. They "hate the sin, love the sinner." They combine correction and punishment with affectionate forgiveness, understanding, and encouragement. They are neither weak nor harsh but rather *affectionately assertive*. They love their children too much to let them grow up with their childish faults and self-centeredness still intact.

(6) When they must correct anyone in the family, they do this personally and privately whenever possible. They try not to chew people out in public.

(7) Mom and Dad never fear being temporarily "unpopular" with their children. The kids' long-term happiness is more important than their present sulking and bruised feelings from correction. The parents are confident that their kids' resentment will soon pass. Someday, please God, the

children will understand and thank Mom and Dad for the love behind their steadfast guidance.

(8) They frequently encourage their children, showing and explaining how to do things right and how to do the right thing. They direct rather than micromanage, and make praise as specific as blame.

(9) They're confident of their authority, which is as great as their responsibility. As parents, they know, they have rights over their children, including their rights to be respected and obeyed. They will not permit their children to infringe on those rights; in a sense, they're prepared to defend their rights against their children's aggression. And they know this lesson has lifelong consequences.

(10) They do not allow rivals in the home to undermine their authority or undo their lessons of right and wrong. They keep the media under discerning control, allowing only what serves to bring the family together.

(11) They understand that they must lead their children to *see the invisible*—those critical but invisible realities that form a great life: *character, conscience, honor, integrity, spirit of service, truth, justice, moral obligations, social obligations, family solidarity, God, grace, the soul.*

(12) They respect their children's freedom and rights. They teach them how to use their freedoms responsibly, and they exercise only as much control as the children need. They set reasonable limits to the children's behavior. They know they must also show that *invisible line separating right from wrong* in a host of situations—the line we cross when we infringe on the rights of others. This includes the parents' rights not to be disobeyed or treated disrespectfully, and God's right not to be offended by sin. Within the lines, children are free; outside the lines, others' rights are violated—and this the parents will not permit.

(13) Mom and Dad share conversation with their children

until they and their kids know each other inside out. They go out of their way to listen to their children and pay close attention to their growth in character. They watch over and guide their children's performance in sports, chores, homework, good manners, and relations with siblings and friends. The know what goes on in their home and inside the growing minds of their children.

(14) Mom and Dad want their children to be active, and they know that all active people make mistakes. They lead the children to learn from their own blunders. They teach them that active life involves sensible risk-taking, and that there's nothing wrong with mistakes if we learn from them.

(15) They set aside fatigue, anxiety, and temptations to slack off, putting duties ahead of self-centered pursuits. They set aside the newspaper to help with homework. They go without TV to set a good example. They let their kids work with them around the house even when they mostly get in the way. Like a good boss, each is always available to help and advise; consequently, children sense their parents would drop anything if they really needed them. They are willing to put off a life of leisure until their children have grown and gone.

(16) They give their children a sense of family history and continuity. They tell stories about grandparents and forebears, people of quiet courage and even heroism.

(17) They let the children know their opinions and convictions about current events and their likely drift, the future world the kids must cope with. They explain, as best they can, the past causes and future implications of present-day affairs. They press their kids to become readers as well, to get out of themselves and see life through the eyes of others.

(18) Mom and Dad are open to the children's suggestions, their "input" about family decisions. After all, it's their family, too. When matters are of little weight, the parents accede to their preferences, let them have their way, or at least let them

have their say. But larger, more important matters are decided by the parents. Mom and Dad will sometimes let children choose, for instance, what dessert to enjoy or what games to play, but the parents decide which school the children attend and which TV programs will enter the house.

(19) When either parent has caused offense, he or she apologizes. Each puts justice and truth ahead of ego.

(20) Habitually, parents punctuate their speech, especially toward each other, with *please, thank you,* and *excuse me.* They lead their children to do the same.

(21) They draw strength and courage from their religious faith and love for their family.

(22) They know that time passes quickly and they haven't much of it. So they make smart use of scant resources. They make the time, even small slivers of it here and there, to live with their children.

(23) Their life as parents is, to them, one of noble, self-sacrificing adventure. As long as the kids are in their care, they will not quit or slacken in their mission to form their children's character for the rest of their lives. No matter what the cost, Mom and Dad will support and provide for each other and for their children. To them, the family is a sacred gift from God— the meaning of their lives, the object of their powers, the center of their hearts.

Children led by parents like this have a fighting chance to become great men and women. They grow to honor Dad and Mom, live by lessons learned since childhood, and then pass these on to their own children whole and intact.

Profiting from Compass Group Discussions

Organizing and running a Compass Group

One of the more vexing problems in modern life is the disappearance of the extended family. This is, as you know, that network of close relations—parents and grandparents, married siblings, aunts and uncles, cousins of all ages and their spouses—that parents relied on for centuries to answer questions, resolve doubts and dilemmas, lend a sympathetic ear, pass on experience, give encouragement and back-up.

What we find today instead is that young parents are isolated, and certainly feel isolated, as never before. Our mobility has scattered us far and wide. Parents and siblings live at a distance. Aunts, uncles, and cousins are often virtual strangers. And, of course, many relatives have huge personal and family problems of their own; they're in no position, alas, to give advice or encouragement to anyone.

For this reason, more and more young couples are organizing themselves into mutually supportive parent groups. What they can't get from relatives, they get from good friends. Meeting with like-minded, interesting friends—that is, people who share the same principles but have different temperaments, backgrounds, and points of view—they discuss family issues and share experiences. They've found the truth in the old adage: "Good friends help us make life's most important decisions."

Almost without exception, couples in these groups found they've enjoyed the experience and received great encouragement from it. What were the benefits they gained from this investment? This is what they've told me. . . .

- They befriended other parents who share their basic values and their dedicated commitment as parents—that is, as one of them put it, "to make the most of our one and only chance to raise our children right."

- They pieced together a much clearer picture of what parents conspicuously lack these days: a clear "job description" of parenthood. After all, kids do not come into the world with a set of instructions, and you get only one chance to do the job right.

- They were pressed to think deeply about the basic issues of family life (thus straightening out priorities) and plan out their children's growth in character. They could see where their family life was headed, and, very important, could more readily and convincingly explain their principles to their children.

- From other people's experience, they received affirmation that they were on the right track. This steeled them to persevere through tangled times, no matter what.

- They learned what's *normal* behavior among kids of different ages. (A lot of parents' indecision comes from not knowing what's normal.)

- They absorbed a lot of detailed practical advice from other parents, especially older "veterans." They often learned (to their relief) that there are various ways of handling problem situations, and they could choose the one that best fit their temperaments. Thus they grew more confident in leading their children.

- They used their own experience to help and encourage other parents as well, especially newlyweds and parents of very young children.

- They drew support from a network of respected friends whom they could call on for advice, or just affirmation and encouragement. No longer did they feel isolated. They could draw strength from the same sort of "peer-group support" that teenagers enjoy. (Very important when the children enter adolescence. If teens can feel confident from peer-support, why can't their parents?)

• Not only did they make good friends, but so did their children. The kids from their families also grew to befriend each other. Later, as teenagers and young adults, they often socialized, dated, and in some cases even married each other.

• In short, they formed the same natural, mutually supportive network of friends that our forebears relied on for centuries to clear up questions and stay on track.

Nearly all discussion groups consisted of couples, both husbands and wives. But some were only for mothers, and others only for fathers. (Dads too need a job description; and men, as much as their wives, enjoy getting together to swap ideas and experiences.) Whatever the composition, here are their experienced tips for anyone organizing a group:

(1) Don't try to do everything by yourself. Start with a steering committee of three couples and divide up the work. Decide on a definite schedule for meetings (see below) and sequence of topics based on this handbook's chapters. Put this plan in writing as a simple informative flyer; the more that details (dates, times, topics) are set in place, the more likely will people decide to join you. Make lists of people who would probably be interested. (Rule of thumb: Count on inviting three times as many people as you hope will show up.) Invite them to an initial informal get-together where you explain the program's purposes and specific details. From those who opt to join, gather their phone numbers and e-mail addresses to keep them informed.

(2) Because many busy parents are understandably chary of open-ended commitments, make clear to prospective participants that the program is not open-ended. That is, there's a definite sequence of six or seven meetings, and if people

prefer to drop out after that, no problem. In fact, people are free to disengage at any point and to rejoin later if they wish: "We're all busy parents, so we understand."

(3) For nearly everyone, Friday or Saturday night once a month, on a set weekend, seems to work best. A fixed night of the month helps people to plan their calendars and remind themselves. The optimal time slot is from 7:00 to 9:00 P.M. (Allow about a half-hour for socializing, and then start at 7:30.) Though sometimes meetings will be a bit late starting, it's important to end on time. At 9:00 sharp, some people will have to leave, while others will stay a while for decaf coffee and snack. For nearly all families, a weeknight is out of the question and Saturday night can also be a problem. (This varies, though. Many couples prefer Saturday night. This is one of the details that the steering committee needs to determine initially.)

(4) Some times of the year are tough for parents to get away. September fills up with start of the school year; late November and all of December conflict with holidays. January through May seems to be the optimal time, though sometimes early October and early November are possible. Because of vacations, the summer is generally unsuitable for discussion groups, though it's fine for other social gatherings like cookouts and picnics for participants. So, the group would meet rather early in the month (say, the second Friday evening) during October, November, January, February, March, April, and May. Some groups arrange a party or family picnic in May or June to end out the year.

(5) Where to host this? Some groups prefer one fixed venue. Others rotate among homes of the steering committee and then, later, other people's homes. The limiting factor seems to be the size of the living room or family room where meetings are held. Generally speaking, the optimal size is six to ten couples. Any more than this, especially without a

strong-willed but tactful moderator, can lead to confusion in discussion.

(6) Set up comfortable seating arrangements, especially for the men. Because of their bodies' higher center of gravity, men need chairs with arm-rests (not benches or straight-back chairs) in order to sit comfortably for an hour or more.

(7) Cost? Mainly the price of this handbook and a couple of dollars for snacks. The cost for the activity itself shouldn't be more than $25, though babysitting charges will add to the total outlay. Whatever the cost, see it as an investment.

(8) What about bringing small children along? Some organizers tried this at first and found it so distracting that they dropped it. Since participants are given plenty of notice, they should be able make their own babysitting arrangements. "Treat it like a monthly night out at the movies," said one organizer, and this seems to be most effective approach.

(9) Format? Encourage people to read (or at least skim) a chapter beforehand and come prepared for questions and discussion. Have one person responsible in advance for leading the discussion; this responsibility can be rotated on a volunteer basis. Be a learner, not just a teacher. Set out with the attitude that you're doing this to cement friendships and to learn how to be a better parent yourself. Maintain a spirit of service. Remind yourself often that, in the long term, you are doing an enormous amount of good for each family involved.

(10) Keep things light and friendly. Use a lot of humor, even with serious topics. Be determined that everyone will have a good time, a pleasant evening. Use the discussions to cement friendships that will last for years. Don't let some participants be heavy-handed or dogmatic. Shun political discussion and religious controversy. Avoid doctrinaire participants (that is, don't invite them in the first place), or tactfully suggest they either tone things down or just disengage from the program.

(11) Stay in touch with participants between meetings, even by phone. Have an occasional social event—party, family picnic, watch a ball game together—during the "off-season."

(12) Don't shoot for big numbers and don't be disappointed by occasional low turnout. If even one family is helped significantly, turns things around for the better at home, the whole effort is worth it.

(13) Keep ongoing notes of experience in order to keep improving.

(14) As time goes on into the second and third year and later, shoot for some variety: discussion questions, videos, reviews of parenting books, short case studies.

(15) Stick with it. It's an investment. Years from now, you and your friends—and your grown children—will be glad you did.